The Story of Bankside

FROM THE RIVER THAMES TO ST GEORGE'S CIRCUS

by Leonard Reilly and Geoff Marshall

London Borough of Southwark 2001
Neighbourhood History No. 7

ISBN 0 905849 31 0
Published 2001

© 2001 London Borough of Southwark

Inside front cover
An aerial view of 1961 of Bankside from the Cathedral (top)
to the Oxo Tower (bottom). Note the half-built power station and
St Christopher House, behind.

Inside back cover.
Southwark Underground Station, the concourse and its wall
of curving blue glass.

Contents

Introduction

CHAPTER ONE:
From first farmers to 18th-century glassmakers:
Bankside 4000BC to AD1750   **5**
First settlers   5
Saxon and medieval Southwark   7
Recreation and entertainment   19
The 17th century   27

CHAPTER TWO:
Bankside 1750-1914:
industry, transport, townscape and government   **35**
An area transformed   35
Bankside at work   47
Local government: shifting responsibilities   63

CHAPTER THREE:
Bankside 1750-1914: people and society   **66**
The charities and institutions of St George's Fields   66
Bankside's social problems   71
Official inaction   78
Reform   79
Education   88
Public safety: the Fire Brigade   93
Churches, cathedrals and chapels   94
Daily life   99

CHAPTER FOUR:
Industrial rise and fall, and the birth of
modern Bankside: 1914-2001   **103**
World War I   103
Improvements following World War I   105
Industrial Expansion after World War I   109
World War II   115
The postwar years   118
Regeneration   131
Tate Modern and other attractions   135

Booklist   143
Index   144

Acknowledgments

I pay grateful thanks to the many people who have helped towards the publication of this book: my co-author Geoff Marshall, who used to work for the Central Electricity Generating Board and is now a member of the excellent body of London Registered Blue Badge Guides, for his words on Bankside's industries and his prompt delivery of his text; Carol Enright, for her design flair and coolness under tight deadlines; my colleagues at Southwark Local Studies Library: Stephen Humphrey, Steve Potter and Lynne Kendall, for their thorough and generous criticism and improvements to the draft text, and for coping with me in the book's increasingly fraught pre-publication days; Mary Boast, for her equally helpful comments; Charles Philips, for lightening and humidifying my dry text; Chloe Bird, for help with research and pictures; Robin Densem, Simon Blatherwick, Karen O'Keeffe, Phil Evans and Martin Cook, for helping with sources and information; Pat Kingwell, for vital equipment; Mark Shingler, for providing a writer's ideal environment and my wife Sarah, for enduring the swings of enthusiasm and stressure and press the whole project has brought.

All these people have ensured the book is much better than it otherwise would have been, but I am sure there are still mistakes – mine.

The quote from *A Dead Man in Deptford* by Anthony Burgess (published by Hutchinson) is by permission of Random House Group Ltd. and the quote from *Policeman's Prelude* by Harry Cole is by kind permission of the author.

I also thank the following for kindly giving permission to use their illustrations: Museum of London front cover; Aerofilms, inside front cover; London Transport Museum/Mr E C Dixon, inside back cover; Peter Froste p.4; National Monuments Record, (English Heritage), p.108; Sainsbury's Archives p.110; South London Gallery, p.113; Alpha Picture Library, p.117; Tate Gallery p.136.

Len Reilly
Southwark Local Studies Librarian
January 2001

London Borough of Southwark Neighbourhood Histories
1   The Story of Camberwell
2   The Story of Dulwich
3   The Story of Peckham and Nunhead
4   The Story of Walworth
5   The Story of Bermondsey
6   The Story of Rotherhithe
7   The Story of The Borough
8   The Story of Bankside

Introduction

Southwark is an ancient riverside area directly across the River Thames from the City of London. Together with Westminster and the City itself, it forms the core of London. This book provides an introduction to the history of the area of the riverside from the OXO Tower in the west to Southwark Cathedral in the east, and south to St George's Circus. Bankside is one of Southwark's oldest streets. Strictly, it is no more than a short street running east-west along the riverfront from Bankend – roughly where the Cannon Street railway crosses Clink Street – to a point between Tate Modern and Blackfriars Bridge. The point where the street ended may seem arbitrary today, but it was an important administrative boundary when the street was first created in the Middle Ages. In addition to the riverfront, this book also discusses the area known as St George's Fields around St George's Circus. The St George in question is that of the parish of St George the Martyr. Bankside is undergoing a rebranding and promotion encompassing an area much larger than its true historic street name. In this book, much of north Southwark west of Borough High Street will be treated as Bankside.

The previous edition of this volume in the Neighbourhood History Series was called *The Story of Bankside* and covered the same area. Like other recent volumes in the Neighbourhood History Series, this book departs from the series' original scheme. While this title still aims to serve as an introduction to the general reader, it is significantly larger than before, deals in more detail with recent times and has the needs of the adult reader in mind.

Information on the area to the east can be found in *The Story of the Borough* and on the area to the south in *The Story of Walworth*. There is some overlap and artificiality in the division between this book and *The Story of the Borough*. This volume discusses the Anglican Cathedral, but not its near neighbours Borough Market or London Bridge, but it does talk about the hop trade, which could be thought part of the history of Borough High Street. Equally the King's Bench Prison, on St George's Fields, and the area known as the Mint are discussed in *The Story of the Borough*.

While the boundaries for Bankside as defined and used here are arbitrary and designed to fit in with the scheme of other books in the series, the definition used for Southwark is a precise one. Today Southwark is one of the 33 London Boroughs and covers a triangular-shaped area from Bankside to Rotherhithe to Dulwich. However, Southwark insofar as this book is concerned is the ancient town of Southwark, which had as its spine Borough High Street and which extended west to the modern Borough boundary, south to the start of the Old Kent Road and east along the river to St Saviour's dock.

In very recent years Bankside has changed hugely and has opened itself to the world. In the eyes of most Londoners and virtually all visitors to London, Bankside is a newcomer on the London scene. In historical terms, too, the area covered by this book was late in developing. Aside from the area at the foot of London Bridge and ribbon developments south along Borough High Street and west along the riverfront, the majority of the area was not developed until the late 18th and early 19th centuries. This was an extraordinarily late start for somewhere very close to London. The reason was that the land was low-lying and marshy and its owners, most importantly the City Corporation, were reluctant to drain it or to provide transport links.

In general terms, historians have neglected Southwark's contribution to London as a whole – they have allowed it to be overshadowed by the achievements of the City, Westminster and the West End. This is not because Southwark has made an inferior or lesser contribution than these areas, but because much of its contribution has been to provide elements that all cities generate but whose existence they prefer to ignore. While the City developed into the country's commercial and financial centre, Westminster into the centre for the Court, the judiciary and later national government and the West End into the place of residence for the country's nobility and gentry, Southwark made no contribution to these worlds of affluence and power. Instead Southwark in general – and Bankside in particular – was the antithesis of the West End, Westminster and the City: unruly, badly run, poor, industrial, overcrowded, immoral, polluted, coarse, raucous, unhealthy.

But Southwark has also been creative, independent, cosmopolitan, tolerant, vigorous, reforming, resilient, enterprising. Over time it has provided a home to London's red-light district, to its theatreland, to a huge range of industries, to many immigrant communities, to criminals seeking sanctuary, to the Victorian poor in overwhelming numbers and, more recently, to a culture-led regeneration that is the envy of London.

Bankside's history falls into three broad but unequal sections. During its early history, roughly up to the end of the 18th century, the area was largely undeveloped apart from the immediate riverfront, where there was much activity. From the 18th century to the early 20th century, there was a period of vigorous development and urbanisation. The riverfront became increasingly industrial and districts to the south were absorbed into the urban whole of Georgian and Victorian London. The later 20th century has seen a gradual decline in industry, a process that advanced very quickly after World War II, and very recent years have seen Bankside become part of central London once again.

A view of Roman London c. AD 75.
Note the islands that made up the settlement of Southwark and the fact
that the location of modern Bankside is flooded marsh.

CHAPTER 1

From first farmers
to 18th-century glassmakers:
Bankside 4000BC-AD1750

Southwark owes its existence to a series of small gravel and
sand islands that once rose slightly above surrounding marshland
on the south bank of the River Thames. The islands provided
the Romans with a dry, secure base from which to cross the river
and reach the higher land opposite where they built the new
settlement of London. In prehistory and during the Roman and
early medieval periods, the Bankside area – except at its extreme
eastern end – had no such geographical advantages. Until the
13th or 14th century, when the first embankments and ditches
were built, the area close to the Thames was marshland that was
inundated at every high tide. Farther inland, the ground was
heavily waterlogged and unsuited to settlement.

FIRST SETTLERS

Evidence for human activity in the Bankside area dates back
6,000 years to the Neolithic period. At that time the level of the
Thames was about 15 feet (5 metres) lower than it is today, so
settlement was easier than in more recent periods. In Hopton
Street, archaeologists have found the remains of a Neolithic
pottery bowl and the marks of a prehistoric plough.

The Romans established Southwark as an urban centre, but
appear to have given it no name distinct from London – or if they
did, the name is now lost. The core of Roman Southwark followed
the higher, dry land along Borough High Street – understandably,
the settlers were less keen to push west into the marsh. In all
probability, the settlement confined itself entirely to the naturally
dry ground: the exact shape of the gravel and sand islands is not
known, but current thinking suggests that the largest, which was
nearest the river, was roughly oval in shape, oriented northeast/
southwest, and measured about 650 yards (600 metres) along its
long axis and 330 yards (300 metres) across.

Recent archaeological work has shown that Roman Southwark was larger and more important economically than was previously thought. At the eastern end of Bankside were a number of large buildings, including one on the site of Winchester Palace, where there was possibly also a bath house. A figurine of a hunter god and part of a sea god have been found beneath Southwark Cathedral, raising the intriguing prospect that the site was used for religious rituals during the Roman period. Commerce and trade were important in Roman Bankside: imported foodstuffs were landed at wharves on the north side of modern Clink Street and hearths found in Park Street indicate that metals were smelted in the area. Remains of a cemetery found at Roman Southwark's periphery near the junction of Park Street and Southwark Street suggest that the Romans followed their usual practice of digging a burial ground at some distance from the town centre.

In general, Roman Southwark restricted itself to the largest island, but there were two exceptions to this in the Bankside area. Firstly, there are remains of Roman revetments – structures built out from the natural shoreline into the river – along the riverfront north of Clink Street; secondly, archaeologists have uncovered evidence for the start of a major road that ran southwest from the bridgehead roughly towards the position of the modern crossing from Lambeth to Westminster.

The Romans left Britain in 410 and without their influence urban settlements in southern Britain eventually collapsed. London and Southwark were abandoned by their inhabitants and languished unpopulated and decaying for centuries. It is not until 914, and a document called the *burghal hideage*, that we again find evidence of a settlement on the south side of the River Thames opposite London. The document contains the first use of the name Southwark – suthringe gewruche ("defensive work of the men of Surrey"): the men of Surrey were defending London and the recently re-established bridge to it from attack by Norse invaders. The burghal hideage describes a whole series of defensive works and forts established across southern England by King Alfred.

SAXON AND MEDIEVAL SOUTHWARK

THE PRIORY OF ST MARY OVERIE – AND THE PARISH OF ST SAVIOUR

St Saviour's Church – previously the Priory of St Mary Overie and later additionally elevated to a Cathedral Church. A view of c. 1750.

The revitalised settlement expanded. *The Domesday Book* of 1086 mentions a monasterium (minster), although its precise location is uncertain and there are no other documents or archaeological remains to substantiate its existence. What is clear is that in 1106 an Augustinian Priory was established. Later this became known as the Priory of St Mary Overie. The name means simply "St Mary's over the water", but there is a legend that the priory was established by Mary, daughter of John Overs, a Thames ferryman. The clergy lived in buildings on the north side of the church. They were ordained priests, who had two important duties: to look after churches in their care and to minister to the sick and poor. Within the priory, they founded a hospital dedicated to St Thomas that would evolve into the modern St Thomas's Hospital.

The most remarkable feature of the priory's long history is that the main building survived at all. A major fire in 1212 necessitated wholescale rebuilding, while three centuries later, in the 1530s, the fabric of the priory survived the dissolution of the religious houses. Henry VIII closed down the religious houses not principally over issues of doctrine, but because he wished to appropriate their wealth and redistribute it for his own political gain. The religious institutions had two major assets: the lands they owned and the fabric of their buildings. Typically, monastic buildings were pulled down very shortly after their dissolution and the materials re-used at other locations. St Mary Overie did not suffer this fate – the building was leased and later purchased by the townspeople and became the town's new parish church, dedicated to St Saviour.

The priory, and later the parish church, maintained a close relationship with the Bishop of Winchester, who lived nearby. After the fire of 1212, Bishop Peter des Roches led work to rebuild the priory and at the Reformation Bishop Stephen Gardiner assisted the townspeople of Southwark in obtaining the lease of the building to make it the town's parish church.

The building as it stands today incorporates many architectural styles. There are round Norman arches and an early English choir and retrochoir. The nave roof collapsed in 1469, was rebuilt in wood and was again replaced in the 19th century. The elaborate and wittily carved roof bosses from the 15th century roof are on display in the building today. In 1520 there were major alterations inside and out when the tower and the carved stone screen behind the high altar were built.

The building faced repeated threats in the 18th and 19th centuries. The parish struggled to raise sufficient funds from their increasingly impoverished inhabitants to maintain such a large building, which was more and more out of place in what had become an intensely urban and overcrowded part of London. In 1830 a chapel at its east end was demolished for the approach to the new London Bridge. The building was again threatened in the 1860s when the railway line from London Bridge to Charing

Cross was built. But in the early 19th century the church was championed by the architect George Gwilt, who was responsible for restoring the choir and retrochoir. The nave and its medieval wooden roof had to be demolished and a temporary structure was put in its place. This was in turn replaced in 1897 when the nave was completely rebuilt to designs by Sir Arthur Blomfield.

The church contains a number of memorials to celebrated people associated with Southwark. John Gower, the poet and a contemporary of Chaucer, is buried there, as is Edmund Shakespeare, brother of William. A memorial to William Shakespeare was erected there in 1912: each year on the playwright's birthday, 23 April, a service is held to celebrate his life and work. There is a separate chapel dedicated to John Harvard, whose collection of books was the nucleus of the library of Harvard University in Massachusetts, USA. Harvard's family owned the Queen's Head Inn on Borough High Street; he left for North America in 1637, aged 30. Launcelot Andrews, the last Bishop of Winchester to live in Southwark, also has his tomb in the church.

In 1905 the Church of St Saviour was made a Cathedral. The most important surviving medieval building in London south of the River Thames, it is central physically, administratively and symbolically to the development of Bankside and of Southwark in general.

PARISHES AND SCHOOLS

The laity of the town worshipped not at the priory but at their parish church. The parish of St Margaret covered most of the Bankside area: the church itself was halfway along Borough High Street, near where the war memorial stands today. A smaller parish, St Mary Magdalen, had its origin in a chapel built against the south side of the priory in the early 13th century. It served as the place of worship for those living between the priory and the high street. By the early 16th century, these two buildings were too small for their parishioners' needs. The parishes amalgamated in 1539, taking a lease on the priory – and later purchasing it – for use as a new and impressively large parish church.

The most ancient educational establishment in Southwark, St Saviour's School, had its origin in the new parish. The idea of creating a grammar school for the parish first appeared in a lease of 1559 taken on the parish church. The school's first permanent home was part of a house in Green Dragon Court, close to the church. The school stayed there until the 19th century, when it moved to Sumner Street. The official date of the school's establishment is 1562, when it received its royal charter, which officially acknowledged its existence and formalised the powers of the governors, giving them permission to own land. The school provided education to 100 boys and the curriculum was overwhelmingly classical in its content; the boys had an examination each September. The pupils were taught by a single master: the first was Christopher Ocland. A St Saviour's School still exists today as a girls' comprehensive in the New Kent Road. The foundation of St Saviour's School was mirrored by the establishment, at about the same time, of St Olave's School in the neighbouring parish of that name on the east side of Borough High Street.

TOWNSCAPE AND POPULATION

Saxon and early medieval Southwark expanded south and east following the higher dry land, but it was not until the 13th century that demand for land was high enough to justify systematic attempts to build embankments against the river and ditches for drainage. The tenants of the two riverside manors – the Bishop of Winchester's, also known as "the Clink", at the eastern end of the district, and Paris Garden to the west – were responsible for embankments, ditches and drains; the manorial authorities attempted to ensure that the necessary work was carried out.

Bankside as a street name was first heard of in the 16th century, but it has its origins in a causeway built alongside the river and first mentioned in 1218. Other surviving street names that allude to the embanking process include Broadwall, which still forms part of the boundary between the modern Boroughs of Southwark and Lambeth and was the embankment to the west side of the manor of Paris Garden; Upper Ground was the riverfront embankment of the same manor.

Floods were frequent and inconvenient – if rarely life-threatening. Crops and pasture on the Bishop of Winchester's estate were often flooded. In addition to embankments, a complex series of ditches and sluices were built. Sixteenth-century maps show a major ditch running parallel to the river and also depict Paris Garden entirely surrounded by ditches. Inland, the most important road running through the district was Maiden Lane, which ran south of and parallel to the river.

The flooding of the River Thames may periodically have threatened Bankside, but locals learned to put its waters to good use. Water mills used tidal power to grind cereals. First the incoming tide powered the wheel, then the water was held in place inland of the wheel by a sluice gate and released when the tide had fallen to power the wheel a second time. There were ten mills on the riverfront at the end of the 12th century, but only one by the mid-16th century. Bankside also had a flourishing leather trade – tanning requires a good supply of water to wash the hides when they are immersed in the tanning pits. From the 14th century onwards, there were three fishponds – the Bishop of Winchester's, the King (or Queen's) and the Great Pike Garden – in which freshwater fish, mainly the aggressive and predatory pike, were bred and farmed for the table. The dyeing of imported cloth and the brewing of ale were other important industries that depended on water.

The River Thames was a main thoroughfare. Goods were landed at wharves and docks on the riverfront. There were two docks: St Mary Overie Dock, a natural inlet at the east end of Clink Street (which is still there) and Moulstrand, a wharf, which was where Tate Modern stands today. Goods were transported by Thames lightermen, a distinct group from the watermen, who carried passengers. The watermen and lightermen were known for their skill – they controlled wherries over 20 feet (6 metres) long and 4 foot 6 inches (1.4 metres) wide – as well as for their quick wit and readiness to fight. It has been calculated that in Elizabethan times there were 3,000 watermen and lightermen working between Westminster and London. The annual Dogget's Coat and Badge race, a rowing race from London Bridge to Chelsea each August, was originally contested only by the watermen and lightermen. It was established in 1721 and is the oldest annually contested event in the British sporting year.

There were a number of important river stairs at which people could alight from the wherries of the watermen. By the middle of the 18th century there were 13, of which the most ancient were St Mary Overie Stairs (at the end of Stoney Street), Falcon Stairs, Paris Garden Stairs and Barge House Stairs. At the very western end of Upper Ground was the Royal Barge House where the ornate ceremonial barges used by monarchs for public processions on the Thames were kept. This barge house was in use during the later 16th century.

It is difficult to establish the population of any place during the medieval and early-modern period and so any conclusions can only be approximate. It is particularly difficult in Southwark, where there was no single administrative unit, and the task is made even harder here as this book discusses only part of the urban whole of Southwark. Historians have estimated that at the time of the Domesday Book in 1086, Southwark's population numbered no more than a few hundred. It increased to about 5,000 in 1300, with Bankside's population (taking this book's arbitrary boundary) standing at less than 2,000. (The most densely populated areas in the town were outside our area, along Borough High Street and Tooley Street.) Along with the rest of the country, Southwark's population fell dramatically during the 14th century as a result the Black Death and migration to other places; in 1381, its total was rather less than half that of 1300.

By the late 15th and early 16th centuries, the population and the town itself had grown rapidly, and, by the middle of the 16th century Southwark's population was about 10,000, with perhaps 3,000 of these in Bankside. Southwark's population continued to increase rapidly throughout the 17th century, from about 19,000 in 1603 to about 25,700 in 1631 and 31,700 in 1678. As Bankside grew it assumed a larger proportion of Southwark's total population, so in 1603 there was probably around 6,500 people in the area, in 1631 8,500 and in 1678 10,000.

Southwark's population relative to that of London grew during the Middle Ages, from perhaps 2 per cent of the total in 1100 to 13 per cent in 1550. There were two main reasons for this. Firstly, by the 16th century London housed as many people as it comfortably could within its boundaries and so the "overspill" lived outside in suburbs, of which Southwark was probably the largest. Secondly, the City authorities prevented individuals they did not want from living or practising a trade within City boundaries – and so Southwark became a popular place for immigrants to settle. A high proportion of London's non-English immigrant population lived in Southwark, making up perhaps 10 per cent of the town's population. The immigrants came largely from the Low Countries – modern Belgium, the Netherlands and western Germany – and were collectively known as "Flemings" or "the Doche". Their presence was only grudgingly tolerated by the established population: popular prejudice dismissed the immigrant men as brewers and the women as prostitutes. This was partly true, but the Doche were also represented in many skilled occupations – for example as cordwainers (shoemakers), haberdashers (traders in cloth), goldsmiths, glaziers and printers. They participated in and developed many of the trades that formed the core of Bankside's industrial base in later centuries.

GOVERNMENT AND MANORS

Unlike the City of London, the town of Southwark never established its own self-governing municipal administration. The City had an elected Council, a mayor, the right to return two MPs and, in theory, a Charter from the Crown confirming these rights. By contrast, the government of medieval and Tudor Southwark was carried out by manorial authorities. The manors were freehold landed estates, in theory held from the Crown, but in practice self-governing in the way they used their lands, dealt with their tenants and administered justice. Residents were answerable to national law in only the most serious criminal cases. The way in which the manors administered their land and dealt with the problems they faced, and the City of London's influence as a powerful and critical neighbour were the key influences that contributed to the character of early Bankside.

The town of Southwark was made up of five manors, four of which feature in the Bankside area. Three were on the riverfront: from east to west, the Guildable Manor, the manor of the Clink and Paris Garden Manor. The Guildable Manor was the smallest and, so far as Bankside is concerned, the least significant. It occupied a very small area immediately around the south end of London Bridge and had a correspondingly small population. The Guildable Manor was owned by the crown and run by officials appointed by the monarch. The other two riverfront manors were much larger and much more important. To the west of the Guildable Manor was the manor of the Bishop of Winchester, later known as the manor of the Clink; further west again was the Templars' Manor, known from the 15th century onwards as Paris Garden Manor. For ease of reference the Bishop of Winchester's Manor will be referred to as the Clink, and the Templars' as Paris Garden, even if the period under discussion is one before these particular names came into use. Inland and south from Bankside was the King's Manor, although it was only known by this name from the 16th century onwards. Much of its land was pasture or marshy waste. The area later became known as St George's Fields.

In very early times the manors of the Clink, Paris Garden and the King's Manor were owned by a single body – Bermondsey Abbey, a large Cluniac Abbey a mile or so to the east of Bankside. The Bishop of Winchester acquired this manor some time before 1180 when Henry of Blois, who was then the Bishop, bought the land from the abbey. In the 1160s Bermondsey Abbey passed the western section of its lands to the Templars. The Abbey retained ownership until the 16th century of what became known as the King's Manor.

There were therefore two unusual elements to the land ownership and administration of early Southwark: firstly, that an urban area the size of Southwark had no charter and town council, and secondly that so much of the land was owned by the Church.

The Clink and the Bishops of Winchester's palace

Many of the prelates of medieval England, including the Abbot of
Battle, the Bishop of Rochester and the Prior of Lewes, had
houses in Southwark. But the palace of the Bishop of Winchester
was the largest and most commanding of all these. After the
Priory of St Mary Overie, the Bishop's Palace complex was the
most important group of buildings in the town. The skeleton of
the ornate rose window of the great hall's west wall still stands.

Winchester Palace was the bishop's London home from c.1150 to
1626. It was visited by the most powerful men in the land, for the
senior clergy of medieval England were as involved with affairs of
state as of the Church and Southwark provided easy access to the
court at Westminster. Thomas à Becket stayed in the palace in
1170 before his final journey to Canterbury; Cardinal Wolsey,
probably the most powerful clergyman of the Tudor period, was
briefly Bishop of Winchester in 1529-30.

The palace was centred on its great hall, which dates from the
early 13th century, with a large series of kitchen buildings to the
west and a chapel and enclosed courtyard to the south. Beyond
this was a walled garden and the rest of the private estate, which
stretched from modern Cathedral Street to modern Great Suffolk
Street. This area – with higher, dry land in its eastern portion –
was the part of Bankside best suited to agriculture: crops were
grown and animals kept here. The garden kept the palace self-
sufficient in foodstuffs up to the 13th century. The modern name
Park Street refers to the manor's park, or walled garden.

In addition to its sumptuous rooms – in which great affairs of
state and church were discussed – the palace also contained one
of the most unpleasant and notorious buildings of mediaeval
Southwark: the Clink prison. A basement below the level of the
high tide that as a result was chronically damp and frequently
flooded, the Clink was unusual, even for a medieval prison, in the
unpleasantness of its accommodation.

The Clink was associated with justice administered locally: it was used to incarcerate offenders against the rules of the manor, sent there by manorial officials. Many of the Clink's inmates were women – Bankside prostitutes – but the prison was also used to jail religious dissenters. For much of the 16th and 17th centuries, England was in a state of religious turmoil and those holding beliefs at variance with those of the government suffered for them. During the reign of Catholic Queen Mary, Protestants such as John Hooper, Bishop of Gloucester, and John Rogers, who published an edition of the Bible in English, were imprisoned in the Clink prior to their execution; in later years, Roman Catholics suffered in the same way.

The more extreme forms of Protestantism found a home in Southwark. Between 1586 and 1592 a group of separatists led by a cleric named John Greenwood and one Henry Barrowe were imprisoned prior to their execution. Their ideas inspired the Pilgrim Fathers who sailed to America in 1620. Nonconformist chapels also established themselves in the area, most notably one in Deadman's Place from 1640 to 1788 and another in Zoar Street, which was established by 1687.

Paris Garden and sanctuaries

Paris Garden Manor was held by the Knights Templars until 1324 when the Templars were dissolved by Edward II. It then passed to the Knights of St John of Jerusalem, popularly known as the Hospitallers. In 1536, the manor came into the Crown's hands. Shortly after that it passed into private ownership and then changed hands more frequently. For much of its early history it was called *Wilds* or *Wideflete*, a reference to its densely wooded character. Many of the trees that grew there were willow trees, a species that thrives in damp conditions. The name Paris Garden first appeared in 1420, but its origin is unknown. Its manor house was in the northeastern corner of the manor. It is probably the same as the balconied building shown prominently on the panorama that is shown on the cover.

Southwark came to have a reputation as a lawless place, due to the number of prisons and the presence of supposed "liberties" and "sanctuaries" – areas in which it was thought criminals could escape justice. Undoubtedly the area did have attractions for the lawless: compared to the City, the town was weakly administered; moreover, it had a fluid population, the City's administration did not extend there so that those pursued by the City's bailiff or sheriff were safe and the large houses offered temptation to the light-fingered.

Part of the claim for lawlessness was the supposed presence of wholesale sanctuary for all criminals. This was not in fact the case. However, in Paris Garden the Knights Hospitallers did use powers, given them by Pope Innocent III, to offer sanctuary to felons. They exercised this right carefully and only for a limited period of time. From the early 15th century onwards, those being pursued for a crime could seek refuge in the manor so long as they registered their presence and obeyed the strict rules imposed on them once there. The area's use in this way attracted the opposition of those nearby, especially the City of London, and the practise of offering sanctuary had declined significantly by the early 1600s.

Left: Winchester Palace: the home of the Bishops of Winchester and centre of activities of the Clink manor. The great hall, whose Rose window still survives, is the long building nearest to the river. A 19th century redrawing of part of the Hollar panorama of 1636-42.

Southwark and the City

The City of London always viewed Southwark with suspicion. Although it recognised the town as a vibrant, active and productive place, and so a potential source of income, it disliked having such a large, autonomous and unpredictable neighbour on its doorstep. The City was frustrated that it could not control Southwark's affairs, especially the activities of which it disapproved, such as uncontrolled tradesmen operating outside the formal and restrictive rules of the City Companies; it also disapproved of Southwark's lawlessness, its brothels and its large number of immigrants from elsewhere in England and from abroad.

The City sought to extend its powers over Southwark and gradually purchased rights of administration there. Key dates in this process were 1327, 1406 (when the City obtained rights of criminal jurisdiction in the Guildable Manor from the Crown) and most importantly 1550, when, for £980, it bought rights of administration in the Guildable, King's and Great Liberty Manors. This purchase was made from the Crown, which had been buying land in Southwark during the early 16th century and had acquired the King's manor at the Reformation. The funds for the purchase came from the City of London's Bridge House Committee, an ancient establishment that administers revenue from City-owned land to maintain Thames bridges that lead to the City. The Clink and Paris Garden manors remained independent of this scheme and continued as autonomous bodies, resistant to the City's disapproval of the way they governed their affairs. Subsequently, the City purchased other lands in Southwark and by the middle of the 18th century was the major landowner in the town.

Despite having substantial power over parts of Southwark, the City's intervention was curiously half-hearted. Southwark became a new ward of the City, called Bridge Ward Without, but uniquely among City wards it had no member representing it on the Court of Common Council, the most important body in the City's administration. Nor did the City seem keen to raise all the revenues it was theoretically due or to use all its administrative powers – presumably because Southwark would cost more to administer properly than it would raise in revenue. As David

Johnson concluded in his book *Southwark and the City,*
Southwark's manorial rights were purchased to "remove the
annoyance of jurisdictional disputes with neighbouring lords".
A piecemeal and highly complex system of administration
developed, which involved the City, the manorial authorities,
the parishes, the County of Surrey and, in the 18th and 19th
centuries, specially formed bodies for particular purposes. These
confusing arrangements were not resolved until the formation of
the Metropolitan Boroughs in 1900.

RECREATION AND ENTERTAINMENT

THE STEWS

Bankside was medieval London's red-light district and Elizabethan
and Jacobean London's theatreland. The red-light district and
theatres became established in Southwark because the City of
London was sufficiently powerful to exclude them from the area it
administered and the weaker, or more tolerant, jurisdiction of the
Clink and Paris Garden allowed them to settle.

Brothels were a feature of Bankside life from the late 13th century
onwards, when the City banned them from its walls. The brothels
were commonly know as "the stews", a reference both to a
contemporary word for the stove that warmed each one, and to
the nearby commercial fishponds. The presence and activities of
the prostitutes featured in local street names. Part of modern
Park Street was previously known as Maiden Lane and there was
also a Love Lane – in the circumstances, both names can only be
seen as ironic. The origin of Cock Lane seems clear enough. The
prostitutes operated from premises, usually inns, along the
riverfront on Bankside. The businesses expanded from seven
stewhouses in 1381 to 18 by 1506.

The stews were in the Clink manor and because of this association
with the Bishop of Winchester, the women were also known as
"Winchester Geese". In seeking to control the stews, the manorial
authorities were hampered by the fact that most of the land on

which the brothels stood was privately owned, having been separated from the rest of the Bishop's estate at a very early date. For the brothel keepers, the prostitutes and their clients, Bankside was a good location: close to London and with easy and discreet access via the boat services of the Thames watermen.

The Bishop as an individual has been portrayed in an unfavourable light for tolerating the activities of the stews and, some have suggested, profiting from them. This portrait is quite unjustified. While it is unusual that the authorities tolerated the stews rather than attempting to suppress them, their regulations were designed to discourage the stewholders and their activities. The power of the brothel keepers was strictly limited, attempts were made to stigmatise and isolate those involved, residents were offered protection from the activities around them and the regulations even offered some protection to the women. The brothel keepers could not advertise under the sign of another trade and were prevented from taking office or participating in wider town life, so safeguarding the town from their influence; they could not own boats, loan money to the women who worked for them, nor hinder their movements. Equally, the women were placed under restrictions: they could not wear aprons (a sign of respectability), nor become stewholders.

The policy of the manorial officers was guided by the realistic view that since they could not be rid of the nuisance they should control it as best they could. However, the regulations were widely flouted. The large number of cases that passed through the manor court and the frequency with which some offenders were presented suggests that some miscreants did not take the court's justice seriously or see its punishments as a sufficient deterrent.

The City complained to Southwark and to the Crown about the nuisance caused by the stews. In 1506 the Crown ordered the closure of the stews, but the decreee had little effect. Henry VIII then made a second order in 1546 and the Bankside stews were closed at that date. However, the problem continued elsewhere – most notoriously in the 17th century at Hollands Leaguer, the building that had been used as Paris Garden's manor house.

The authorities disapproved of the stews not only for moral reasons but also because of wider law and order problems such as drunkenness, violence, theft, harassment of innocent parties and the threat to property of large groups of lively young men in a densely built-up urban area. The last reason also set the City authorities against another form of recreation and entertainment that developed in the later years of the 16th century – bull- and bear-baiting rings and theatres.

THE THEATRES AND BULL AND BEAR BAITING

The earliest theatres in London date from the 1570s, but the City expelled them, fearing threats to public order. For about 20 years from the late 1590s onwards, Bankside was London's theatreland, but it was not a place of exclusively high-brow culture as the activities of the theatres and the bear rings were inextricably linked. They shared buildings, owners, promoters and audiences.

There were four Bankside theatres – the Rose, the Swan, the Globe and the Hope – owned and managed by two fiercely competing companies. The theatres were purpose-built, sharing a round, or almost round, shape that held maximum audience for minimum area and was ideal for secondary use as a bear ring (see below). In constructing new buildings the promoters took a considerable risk: not only did they have to make major financial outlay without guarantee of success, but they also put themselves and their actors within the remit of the restrictive vagrancy laws. They took the risk because they had to – there were no existing buildings suitable for use as theatres. Although inns had been used in the past, innkeepers were increasingly reluctant to become involved in the theatre world, recognising the possibility of prohibition.

The two rival companies were the Admiral's Men under Philip Henslowe and later Edward Alleyn and the Lord Chamberlain's Men, later the King's Men, under the brothers Cuthbert and Richard Burbage. Bankside was not the only place in which they performed plays, as private performances were given at the homes of the aristocracy. The patronage given by the aristocracy

Theatreland. Bankside 1636-42 showing the Globe Theatre and one of the bear rings. But note that the labels are incorrect; the Globe is farther from the river. The view also shows that inland Bankside very quickly gave way to open space An extract from the Hollar panorama.

is reflected in the companies' names and it in part protected the companies from the vagrancy laws that continually threatened their actors' livelihood.

The circular or near-circular theatres were up to 100 feet (30 metres) in diameter and up to three storeys in height. The stage was at ground level in the central well, although actors used other parts of the structure as the play dictated; the rest of the ground level was for the audience. Those in this section were called "the groundlings", and were the most critical and rowdy section of the audience. The theatres were built on a wooden frame with a thatch roof over the outside walls, but the centre of the structure was open to the elements. Performances were held during daylight hours, using natural light; the open-roof design meant that in bad weather the stage and the audience could get wet.

The groundlings stood during the performance, and paid 1d admission (about 20 per cent of a daily wage), while the rest of the audience sat in the galleries and paid 2d or 3d for admission. The theatres were, by our standards, dangerously overcrowded. The Rose had a capacity of 2,500; in comparison, the modern rebuilt Globe has a capacity of 1,500 in a much bigger space.

The Rose was the earliest Bankside playhouse. It stood on a site just north of Park Street at its junction with Rose Alley. It operated from 1586 to 1606 and was built on land leased by Philip Henslowe in 1585. It was a 14-sided polygonal structure built by John Griggs. The stage was enlarged in 1592. The Swan was in Paris Garden, near the north end of modern Hopton Street. It was in operation from 1596 to around 1632 and is known to have been performing plays between 1596 and 1601. Like the Rose, the Swan was managed by Philip Henslowe; it was modelled physically on the Rose.

William Shakespeare and the Globe

The Globe stood just south of modern Park Street, just east of where it runs underneath Southwark Bridge Road. It is the most celebrated of the Bankside theatres because it was part-owned by William Shakespeare and many of his plays were performed there. Built in 1599 from the timbers of another theatre, called the Theatre, which had stood in Shoreditch, the Globe was managed – and part-owned – by Richard and Cuthbert Burbage. It was destroyed by a fire in 1613 – the thatched roof was set alight by a cannon ball fired during a performance of Shakespeare's Henry VIII. The theatre was rebuilt the following year. The Hope was built in 1614 and was owned and managed by Philip Henslowe; later Edward Alleyn took over as its manager. It was also used as a bear ring. The theatres were closed by a government order made in 1642.

Some of the most celebrated plays in the English language were written for the Bankside theatres: many of Shakespeare's plays – including *Hamlet, Othello, Macbeth* and *King Lear* – had their first public performances at the Globe; Christopher Marlowe's *Dr Faustus* had its first performance at the Rose; Ben Jonson's *Bartholomew Fair* was performed at the Hope. While the work of many of the playwrights has survived and is revered today, much of what was written was the 17th-century equivalent of modern TV soap-operas and is justifiably rarely seen today. The playwrights had a prodigious output. Shakespeare's tally of 37 titles over 23 years is meagre when set against that of Thomas Dekker, who was involved in the writing of 32 plays in just two years.

Did Shakespeare live in Bankside? The question has often been asked. He certainly spent long periods of time in the area and is likely to have had lodgings there, but there is no surviving documentary evidence to show that he was a resident. Other members of the Jacobean theatre world were involved personally in the area. Most prominent of these was Edward Alleyn, Philip Henslow's lead actor and son in law. Alleyn was a Southwark resident and, as a warden of St Saviour's Church, was active in other aspects of the town's life. He purchased the manor of Dulwich in 1605 and in 1619 established an almshouse for ten poor people from St Saviour's parish and a school there for boys from St Saviour's parish that has evolved into modern Dulwich College.

In his 1993 novel *A Dead Man in Deptford,* which fictionalises the life of playwright and poet Christopher Marlowe, Anthony Burgess gave a highly evocative picture of Elizabethan Bankside. The Rose, he suggested, smelt of paint and the armpits of the groundlings:

> *"It lay between the bearpit and the bullpit, which resounded with snarls and the tearing of collops of flesh of the baiting dogs that yelped their descant ... The blood let on stage of The Rose was in manner of a second letting, blood already let of pigs and enclosed in bladders themselves enclosed in the garments of our players who, in the comedy of killing, must gush out their lives to the mob's applause ... Any beyond our noise was the noise of dogs and bears and the imagined noise of them that came to their blissful dying in the trugging house of Henslowe."*

Bull and bear-baiting
The bull and bear rings both pre- and post-dated the theatres. The bear rings first appeared in the 1550s. In them bulls, bears and occasionally horses were "baited" – tethered to a post in the centre of a ring, while specially bred dogs were let loose on them.

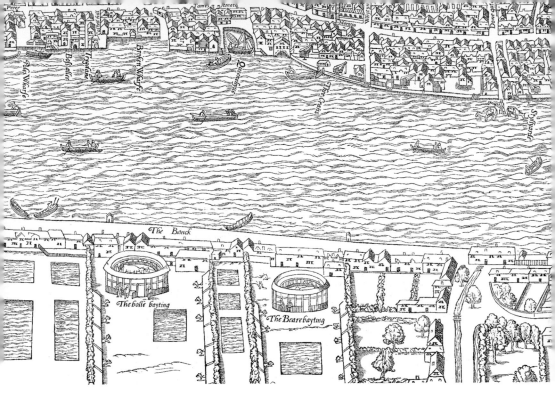

Bankside 1560-70 showing a bull and bear ring (with the dogs leashed in their kennels), riverside stews, fish ponds and a drainage ditch; all key features of early Bankside. An extract from the Agas map.

Spectators placed bets on the outcome. Although barbaric to our tastes, the baiting of animals was hugely popular and was described by contemporaries in approving tones.

There were fewer bull and bear rings than theatres – at no time were there more than two rings – but they were just as popular as the theatres; as enterprises, they were less risky and more profitable than the theatres, and the income they provided was essential to the theatre company managers. The first reference to the baiting of animals is in 1546 – ironically in a weak attempt to suppress it – and the sport is mentioned frequently thereafter. Initially it took place on Sunday afternoons but from the early 1600s onward the day was less fixed. The basic structure needed was no more than an animal-proof round enclosure that allowed the spectators a good view and kennels for the dogs. Two bear rings are shown on the Agas map of 1553, on a site just east of where the modern reconstructed Globe Theatre now stands. At first the rings were no more than circles of vertical poles in the ground but later the structures became more permanent and the Hope Theatre doubled as an animal ring for part of the week. The theatre managers were involved in bear baiting because it guaranteed them an audience and because the office of Master of the Royal Game of Bulls and Bears (a royal appointment) brought status and a sure income. Edward Alleyn and Philip Henslowe were jointly given this position in 1604 and it is significant that their theatrical developments did not start until after this date.

The bear rings may have closed temporarily after the government banned them, together with theatres, in 1642. But they were soon back in business. The last bear ring stood on the east side of Bear Gardens. It was called "Davis' baiting ring" and was in operation from 1662 onwards; it was also a venue for prize fighting . In 1666 Samuel Pepys said of a visit to it that he "saw some good sport of the bull's tossing of the dogs – one onto the very boxes. But it is a very rude and nasty pleasure." The last mention of a bull or bear ring is in 1682.

INNS, ALE AND OTHER ENTERTAINMENT

Throughout its history Bankside has been associated with the brewing industry. The miller summed it up in Chaucer's *Canterbury Tales:*

> *"and if the words get muddled in my tale,*
> *just put it down to too much Southwark ale."*

Each alehouse would have done its own brewing; in the days before hops and the longer life they brought to beer, the drink was for immediate consumption. Before the introduction of hops beer was flavoured with herbs or spices. In 1562 the Venetian ambassador described London beer as "healthy but sickening to taste" and "cloudy like horse's urine".

Later, in the 17th century, dramatist Thomas Dekker wrote of Bankside: "the whole street is a continual alehouse". The riverfront inns and taverns were numerous and further contributed to the area's reputation for high spirits and low life. Prominent among them were the "Castle on the Hoop", on the site of the modern "Anchor", the "Cardinal's Hat", whose existence is recalled in the alleyway of similar name and the "Falcon". The "Falcon" was one of the most important and was on Upper Ground in Paris Garden. It has given its name to a glassworks, a wharf and a modern block of flats.

Frost fairs were a regular, if infrequent, feature of Bankside life until the 19th century. With generally colder winters and a more slowly moving Thames upstream of London Bridge, the river often froze in hard weather. All manner of attractions gathered on its surface, including booths selling food and drink, a bull ring, dancing, braziers for roasting meat and, on one occasion, a printing press. Fairs took place in 1309-10, 1607-08, 1621, 1677, 1683-84, 1715-16 and 1739-40.

THE 17TH CENTURY

Bankside changed significantly in the 17th century, becoming more built-up and an industrial centre. The factors prompting this change were the increasing size and population of London and the departure of the Bishop of Winchester and the break up of his estate. New roads were laid out on what had been the bishop's estate and even the palace's great hall was partitioned and let. Most of the buildings in Southwark were wooden and so fire was always a threat. Disaster struck the district in 1676 when a fire that started in the cellar of an oil shop in Borough High Street destroyed 500 houses.

INDUSTRY

There had always been some industrial activity on Bankside: fishponds, milling and brewing provide good examples. After the death in 1626 of Launcelot Andrews, the last Bishop of Winchester to live in the area, the process of industrialisation accelerated. This was further assisted by the closure of the theatres and the diminishing activity of the bull and bear rings after 1642. These events gave industrialists access to land close to

London and Southwark's cheap and plentiful labour market. Riverfront wharves and warehousing developed, especially to the river side of Upper Ground. By 1750 coal and timber yards stood where houses had once been.

Southwark, and Bankside in particular, was once famous as a centre of the glass industry. Glass is made by fusing sand and limestone with sodium carbonate added as an alkaline flux to lower the melting point. In medieval times wood ash provided the alkaline flux, with wood also used as fuel for the furnace. Wood was a valuable commodity, used extensively in ship building, and this prompted James I, in 1615, to issue a Royal Proclamation forbidding its use as fuel in glassmaking. Coal had to employed instead and this posed real problems for the ancient Wealden glass industry. But the Weald's problem was Bankside's opportunity. Coal could be brought in easily on the Thames and there was a ready market for the finished product in the City of London.

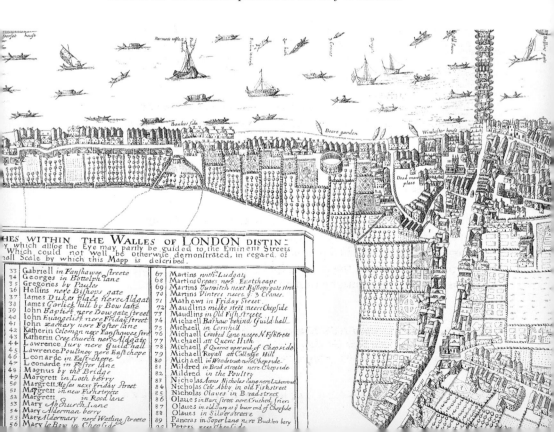

HES WITHIN THE WALLES of LONDON DISTIN:
y which allſoe the Eye may partly be guided to the Eminent Streets
Which could not well be otherwiſe demonſtrated, in regard of
all Scale by which this Mapp is deſcribed.

33	Gabriell in Fanſhawes ſtreete	67	Martins with Ludgate
34	Georges in Bottolph lane	68	Martins Organs nere Eaſtcheape
35	Gregories by Paules	69	Martins Outwitch next Byſhops gate ſtre
36	Hellins nere Biſhops gate	70	Martins Vintree neere y. 3 Cranes
37	Iames Dukes place nere Aldgat	71	Mathews in Friday ſtreet
38	Iames Garlick hill by Bow lane	72	Maudlins milke ſtret neere Chepſide
39	Iohn Baptiſt nere Dowgate ſtreet	73	Maudlins in Old Fiſh ſtreete
40	Iohn Euangeliſt nere Friday ſtreet	74	Michaell Baſhaw behind Guild hall
41	Iohn zachary nere Foſter lane	75	Michaell att Cornhill
42	Katherin Coleman nere Fanſhawes ſtr	76	Michaell Crooked Lane neere N Fiſhſtreet
43	Katherin Cree church nere Aldgate	77	Michaell attr Quene Hith
44	Lawrence Iury nere Guild hall	78	Michaell y Quarne vper end of Chepſide
45	Lawrence Poultney nere Eaſtchepe	79	Michaell Royall att Colledge Hill
46	Leonarde in Eaſtcheepe	80	Michaell in Woodſtreet nere Chepſide
47	Leonarde in Foſter lane	81	Mildred in Brod ſtreete nere Chepſide
48	Magnus by the Bridge	82	Mildred in the Poultry
49	Margrett in Loth berry	83	Nicholas Acons Nicholas lane nere Luberſtret
50	Margrett Moſes next Friday ſtreet	84	Nicholas Cole Abby in old Fiſhſtreet
51	Margrett in new Fiſhſtreete	85	Nicholas Olaues in Breadſtreet
52	Margrett in Rood lane	86	Olaue s in Hart ſtreete nere Cruched friers
53	Mary AtChurch lane	87	Olaues in old Iury at y lower end of Chepſide
54	Mary Alderman berry	88	Olaues in Silverſtreete
55	Mary Aldermary nere Watling ſtreete	89	Pancras in Soper lane nere Bucklers bery
56	Mary le Bow in Chepſide		Peters nere Paul

Vice Admiral Sir Robert Mansel had a monopoly on glassmaking at the time with his patent for making "all sorts of glass with pit coal". He was prevented from building glasshouses in the City because the smoke from coal burning had always been opposed by the clergy and City Fathers – a man was hanged for burning coal in the 13th century! But regulation south of the river was lax and so Bankside was an obvious choice. Accordingly, in 1613, the first coal-fired furnace began production in the precincts of Winchester Palace in a building previously used as a brewhouse. Glassmaking continued for many years at this site until manufacture stopped when the area, known as Glasshouse Yard, was cleared for the construction of the Borough Fruit and Vegetable Market.

There were other glasshouses in the vicinity of St Saviour's Church which could have been in operation as early as Tudor times, making window glass. In the 1670s they were owned by Captain Thomas Morris and glass bottles were made there. These were made using the ancient skill, introduced by the Romans, of glass blowing. A metal pipe was dipped into molten glass and a quantity collected on its end that was then blown into a mould of preformed shape. Bottle glass was usually of poor quality and often coloured green because of iron impurity.

John Bowles was a well known Bankside glassmaker. He had works, opened in 1678, at the junction of Deadman's Place (now Park Street) and Stoney Street and other glasshouses in the Bear Garden, close to the site of the Rose Theatre. It was at the Bear Garden Glasshouse that Bowles, in 1691, pioneered the use of Crown Glass for the manufacture of window panes.

Until the mid-19th century most window glass was made by Bowles' Crown method. The skilled glassblower would blow a hollow glass globe attached to a metal rod or pontil. The glass was then reheated and the pontil rapidly spun so that the glass collapsed about the pontil by centrifugal force into a flat disc.

Left: The Newcourt map of 1658. Note the numerous drainage ditches and the one remaining Bear Garden. Bankside appears to be a narrow peninsula of development, but some of the important inland streets, such a Maid Lane, are not shown.

After further treatment by heat to strengthen them, the panes of glass were cut from the disc. The blemish in the centre where the pontil was attached became the "bull's eye" pane often seen in old windows. Window glass panes were restricted in size: the maximum that could be made was only 24 by 15 inches (60 by 40 centimetres). This accounts for the panes in old buildings being so small. The name of Crown Glass comes from Bowles' trade mark – a crown that he embossed in the centre of each pane. Bowles was soon to move his operations north of the river to Ratcliffe but his Bear Garden Glasshouse was taken over by a syndicate who also made window glass and obtained a patent for "casting glass and particularly looking-glass plates, much larger than was ever blown in England or any foreign parts".

There were further glasshouses on the site of Tate Modern. These were run by the Jackson family, well known glassmakers who also had works as far away as King's Lynn. It was Francis Jackson, born in Bridgnorth in 1659, who in 1688 built the first Cone Glasshouse in Bankside. These were large brick-built structures, 80 feet (24 metres) in height and 40 feet (12 metres) across. The furnace was in the centre and the glassworkers worked in the annular space within the cone in teams of men known as "chairs". The team leader was known as the "gaffer", the first use of this now well known word.

Glassmaking at Apsley Pellatt's Falcon Glassworks.
From Curiosities of Glassmaking *by Apsley Pellatt.*

Lead crystal or flint glass was introduced to London by George Ravenscroft in 1675 and it was soon made in Bankside. Crushed flint and lead oxide were used in place of lime and the finely worked glass was used for domestic ware. In 1693, at their Falcon Glasshouses to the east of Gravel Lane, Francis Jackson and John Straw were making "the best and finest drinking glasses and curious glasses for ornament".

The glassmakers were not universally popular. Bankside women took in laundry from rich merchants across the river and did not take kindly to soot from the glasshouses falling on their clean washing. They even petitioned the king in 1688 that "one John Straw and others are erecting glasshouses in the middle of the parish to the utter ruin of many of the inhabitants whose livelihood depends upon washing". The Jackson dynasty came to an end in Bankside in 1752 and there were a succession of owners at Falcon Stairs including Pellatt and Green, who later opened other works at Upper Ground.

Pellatt and Green, "Glass Makers to the King", became famous the world over for their superb cut glass and cameo encrustation. Such was the quality of their glass that physicist and chemist Michael Faraday carried out research into optical glasses at their works.

The most eminent member of the family was Apsley Pellatt IV, who entered the Falcon works in 1810 and during the following years took out many patents on improved methods of glassmaking as well as publishing books on the subject. Pellatt's cameo encrustations were medallions or other ornaments enclosed in glass and, in his own words, "like the fly in amber they effectively resist for ages the destructive action of the atmosphere". Highly suitable as commemorative records in the foundation stones of new buildings, they have been found as far afield as Philadelphia, USA. In this country, Pellatt's inscribed slabs were placed in Windsor Castle at the time of Wyatville's restoration, in the Wellington Barracks at the Tower of London and in the Royal Exchange. Pellatts moved north of the Thames at the end of the 19th century to bring glassmaking in Bankside to a close.

In addition Montague Close, right next to St Saviour's Church was the centre for the manufacture of English Delftware – tin-glazed pottery, made for every-day use in the kitchen and for eating. This site was the most important and most long lasting in Southwark being in use 1625-1760. There were other kilns in Horseshoe Alley, Bear Garden and Gravel Lane. As well as pots, jars, mugs and other domestic ware the potters also made tiles and other items for use in building. The open spaces were also put to good use, as they became tenter grounds – areas where newly-woven cloth was stretched on hooks to even its texture, or washed cloth was left to dry.

During the English Civil War and Commonwealth or interregnum of 1640-60, the Parliamentarians built a series of wooden forts around London. They were erected in 1643 after King Charles had been forced to flee and were designed to frustrate his army's return. Two of these wooden forts were built on St George's Fields, one near the "Dog and Duck" tavern and the other near Blackman Street (the southern part of modern Borough High Street). The forts were connected by a line of trenches and earthworks.

CHARITIES AND SCHOOLS

Parochial charities provided care and help to the poor, elderly and sick in Southwark. Typically, the charities were established by individuals who in their wills left property or money that was used to raise the necessary revenue; the charity usually took the name of the founder. Many new charities were established in the 17th century – by 1750 there were 36 individually named charities. Most individuals in fact left their property to the parish and so arrangements for carrying out their charitable wishes lay with the Corporation of Wardens, which ran parish affairs.

The largest bequests were made to establish almshouses. The most important of these was also the earliest: established by Queen Elizabeth I in 1584 to provide a home for 14 poor men and assisted by land given by Thomas Cure, it became known as "Cure's College" – the word "college" did not at that time have any link with education. Other almshouses were smaller, providing a home for only two inmates; many charities, such as Emerson's of 1620 or

Cure's College, Park Street. A photograph of before 1862; at that date the almshouses were demolished to make way for a railway extension.

Buckland's of 1628, provided goods, coals or money. Some were idiosyncratic in their requests, such as that of Thomas Emerson, who specified that those receiving his bequest should preferably be related to him or hold the same surname as he did.

Schooling became more widely available in the 17th century. In 1675 Elizabeth Newcomen established a charity school in her name, providing schooling and clothes for poor boys and girls from the parish – one-third specifically from the Clink area. The Zoar Street Presbyterian chapel also had a school. In the early 18th century, both St Saviour's and Christ Church founded parish schools: St Saviour's in 1704 and Christ Church in 1713 for boys and 1719 for girls. St Saviour's Grammar School also expanded: its premises had been destroyed in the fire of 1676 and were replaced by larger, purpose-built ones. It also established a so-called "English school" – to distinguish it from the classical curriculum of the grammar school – for 30 poor boys from the parish.

A NEW PARISH: CHRIST CHURCH

The most significant event in the town's expansion was the
creation of a new parish, of Christ Church, which was taken from
the western portion of St Saviour's parish and which was
coterminous with the manor of Paris Garden. Even though Paris
Garden was still overwhelmingly rural, even in the mid-17th
century, there had been new building and industries especially
along the riverfront and the population had increased. Inland it
had changed little; there was the manor house and another
property, Copt Hall, a little back from the river, and the roadway of
Gravel Lane, but otherwise the area was poorly drained pasture.

Two factors prompted the creation of the new parish. Firstly, the
growth in population and the number of new buildings meant
St Saviour's was too far distant to be convenient for many
worshippers. Secondly, John Marshall – a local resident whose
name is associated with many parochial charities in Bankside –
left £700 in his will for the erection of a new parish church. He
died in 1631 but the new church was not built until 1671. It was
erected on land in the centre of the manor given by William
Angell, the largest landowner in the area, who was developing
land he owned. The process incurred opposition from St Saviour's.
The new church had been built with insufficient foundations for
the marshy ground on which it stood and within 50 years it was
said to be falling down. A new, larger and more robust church was
built and was complete by 1741. It is unusual that a new parish
was formed by a charity and in later years there was tension and
confusion between the role and powers of the charity, which had
the right to appoint the incumbent, and the church's developing
civil responsibilities.

CHAPTER 2

Bankside1750-1914:

Industry, transport, townscape and government

If in 1750 a time traveller who had known Bankside in the medieval period had revisited it, he or she would have seen many features familiar from medieval times. But the same traveller visiting again 100 years later would have found the area utterly unrecognisable.

AN AREA TRANSFORMED

THE DEVELOPMENT OF ST GEORGE'S FIELDS

In 1750 Bankside was just starting to change from its early form. The majority of buildings were still in the northeastern corner of the district, on land owned by or leased from the Bishop of Winchester. Farther west, development followed the river along the streets called Bankside and Upper Ground. There were also newer, ribbon-type developments along ancient streets slightly inland, such as Gravel Lane (modern Great Suffolk Street), Green Walk (Hopton Street), Maid Lane (Park Street) and Broadwall. Ancient embankments and drainage ditches were still very much in evidence. Farther inland the King's Manor was barely touched by new building. This area became known as St George's Fields, as it was in the parish of St George the Martyr. It was an area of about 150 acres of unenclosed, marshy strip fields that was used as Southwark's common.

By 1850 all the open space in the riverside area had been infilled and evidence of the drainage ditches had gone. But the most dramatic changes had taken place in St George's Fields. These were no longer fields but an overwhelmingly urban mixture of houses, roads, institutions and factories. What is extraordinary is not the extent of this change – there are many examples of equally dramatic change taking place in the same, or shorter, periods in many other parts of London – but that an area no more than one mile from the city and Westminster had remained undeveloped for so long. As a comparison, by 1750 Mayfair,

Holborn, Shoreditch and Ratcliff (the old name for Wapping) were all already established suburbs of London.

St George's Fields was largely under the control of the City of London and its Bridge House Committee. The City had rights of administration, which it had purchased in 1550, and the Bridge House Committee owned much of the land. St George's Fields was part pasture, part marshy waste; for some months of the year the fields were cultivated and for the rest they were given over to common grazing. Even in the late 18th century, the shapes of the plots still reflected their medieval origins – they were generally long rectangles, or strips, the typical shape of fields in the Middle Ages. It is extraordinary that a system of agriculture based on a large unenclosed field with strip plots could have survived until the early 19th century so close to London. Landowners distinguished their sections by boundary stones. A network of paths traversed the fields, but because of poor drainage they were difficult to use in wet weather. In addition there was one road across the fields, connecting Newington Butts with Lambeth. Only a handful of buildings stood on the fields in the mid-18th century: in the southwestern corner was the "Dog and Duck" inn and pleasure garden and in the northeastern corner was the King's Bench prison with a windmill nearby. The prison had been built in 1758, when it moved from a site on Borough High Street; the windmill was demolished in 1773.

As St George's Fields was one of the largest open spaces close to London it became a popular place for recreation. It was used for archery practice – able-bodied men could be called to serve in a militia in time of war and so practising archery was an important duty for all, as well as a sport for some. The fields were also a gathering point. It was there in 1660 that Londoners greeted King Charles II on his return from exile and then accompanied him in a procession into London. Not all gatherings were so law-abiding, however. In May 1768, 20,000 people gathered outside the King's Bench prison to demand the release of the radical opportunist campaigner and politician John Wilkes, who was being held inside. Wilkes had been locked up for an alleged libel, although his supporters believed it was to prevent him from furthering his political aims. Troops were called to disperse the mob and about ten of Wilkes's supporters were killed.

In 1780 the Gordon rioters met on St George's Fields and started on their four-day rampage through London. The rioters were so called because they were followers of Lord George Gordon, who had galvanised support to protest against the repeal of laws against Roman Catholics. About 60,000 people gathered with the intention of presenting a petition to Parliament. When in London, however, the crowd's discipline deteriorated – attacks were made on churches and schools used by Roman Catholics and on the homes of those associated with the Catholic Relief Act. The crowd controlled London for four days; its most notorious act was the release of prisoners from most of London's prisons. The King's Bench was opened and burned, as was the Clink, freeing the inmates. This was the last episode in the Clink's history; it never reopened.

The "Dog and Duck" tavern at the fields' southwestern corner was first heard of in the mid-17th century, and was run by a family named Hedger from the 1780s onwards; successive generations of the family would feature in the history of the area over the next 60 years. The "Dog and Duck" was so called because the shapes of the three ponds near it were said to resemble these creatures. The tavern started its life as a refreshment house, but came to prominence and profit through the energy of the Hedger family and the fortunate fact that it was near a source of what passed for fresh water. This enabled it to capitalise on the 18th-century craze for mineral-water spas. Its role in this respect is discussed in Chapter 3; what is important here is that the family leased the property from the Bridge House Estate, and used profits from the tavern to expand into other activities on St George's Fields.

St George's Fields remained an undeveloped open space both because the area was isolated from London – it lacked roads and access to convenient crossing points over the River Thames and because it was undrained. The City of London and the Bridge House Estate took the initiative in removing both of these disadvantages during the sixty years from 1760.

Bridges and roads
The first stage in this process of development was the laying out of roads to connect with the new bridges over the River Thames. Until 1750 the only crossing of the Thames in the London area

was London Bridge. In that year, however, a new bridge was opened at Westminster. Traffic from the bridge heading eastwards to Southwark or the Kent Road crowded onto the only existing road across St George's Fields. This road was widened and developed into what is now called St George's Road. In addition, a new road was built, starting as an extension to Westminster Bridge Road and continuing as Borough Road. It joined Blackman Street (the southern part of modern Borough High Street) almost opposite Newington Sessions House at Horsemonger Lane. The eastern portion of the road was named Borough Road.

In 1760 a second new bridge across the Thames was suggested to connect the western portion of the City of London with Southwark; it became Blackfriars Bridge. The City of London's Bridge House Committee proposed the idea of a new bridge and gave the task of carrying out the work to the committee's chief surveyor Robert Mylne.

The bridge was to enter Southwark halfway along Upper Ground, in Christ Church parish, at the point where Marygold Stairs had

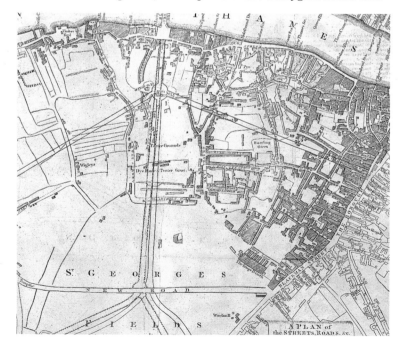

THE STORY OF BANKSIDE

provided access to the river. On its north side, the bridge linked into the network of crowded streets in the City through a new road built along the line of the Fleet River. (It was probably the ease with which this northern approach could be built that determined the bridge's position.) On the south side, the planners were faced with an abundance of open space through which to provide a link with existing roads. How this should be done was the subject of a number of proposals. The agreed plan involved building only one road, running due south from the bridge foot and terminating in a junction with Westminster Bridge Road. This junction, which became St George's Circus, was situated on land that was slightly higher and so better drained.

Parliament approved the proposals in 1769 and construction began shortly afterwards; the road was completed and carrying traffic only one year later. It was called Great Surrey Street, and was renamed Blackfriars Road in 1829. In 1770 the Bridge House Committee suggested that an obelisk be built at St George's Circus; the suggestion was agreed on and the obelisk was in place by 1771. The crest of the City of London was carved on it, along with an inscription saying it was built during the mayoralty of Brass Crosby. The obelisk remained in the middle of St George's Circus until 1905, when it was replaced by an ostentatious, but short lived, clock tower. The obelisk was moved to the grounds of the Bethlem Hospital, but was returned to its original position in 1996.

In the early 19th century two further bridges were built across the Thames and their newly built southern approach roads both ran through the area. Waterloo Bridge (originally called Strand Bridge) was opened in 1817 and a new road was built to link it to Westminster Bridge Road. This was called Waterloo Road; it joined Westminster Bridge Road very near its junction with St George's Circus. Like Blackfriars Road, it was a distinguished, wide boulevard.

Left: One of the many plans drawn up for the new road to connect Blackfriars Bridge with the surrounding area. The roads running almost directly from the bridge foot to Lambeth and Southwark were never built. Notice just how bare St George's Fields was.

The final new main road was Southwark Bridge Road, but it was not as impressive as its predecessors. It was built to connect Southwark Bridge, which opened in 1819, with Newington Causeway. As with Blackfriars Bridge, the line of the river crossing for Southwark Bridge was determined by the ease of building the approach on the City side of the river – in this instance Queen Street. On the Southwark side the new road cut through a built-up area and had to meander to avoid businesses and homes. Again as with Blackfriars Bridge, the building of Southwark Bridge caused the destruction of ancient river stairs, in this instance Horseshoe Alley Stairs. Southwark Bridge Road wove an intricate course between the Anchor Brewery and Potts' Vinegar works, then followed largely open land until it merged for a short distance with Little Guildford Street, just south of its junction with Union Street. It then swung southwest to avoid the King's Bench Prison and crossed Borough Road before terminating at Newington Causeway.

The new roads ran too far south of Southwark to relieve the pressure of traffic on Borough High Street and the parish of St Saviour agitated for a new road to link Borough High Street with Blackfriars Road: it became Union Street. Its construction involved little more than widening and straightening the existing Union Street, Queen Street and Duke Street. Only Charlotte Street, which joined with Blackfriars Road, was genuinely new. Charlotte Street continued beyond Blackfriars Road to form the east end of what is today called The Cut.

New roads and railways in the later 19th century
It was not until the later 19th century that other new roads were built through the area. They were strategic main roads built to serve the transport needs of London as a whole, but they brought destruction and disruption to the local population. The most significant was Southwark Street, which was built by the Metropolitan Board of Works (MBW) in 1864. The road had two functions: to link Borough High Street and Blackfriars Road (thus superseding the inadequate Union Street) and to act as the cover for a subway that carried water and gas pipes and the main sewer. The laying out of Southwark Street required the demolition of 400 houses, making probably ten times that number of people homeless. Southwark Street became the new commercial centre of

Southwark, with offices fronting the street and warehouses behind. Most of the surviving Victorian buildings are built in a bulky, muscular, ostentatious Victorian Romanesque and Gothic style that makes extensive use of brick decoration. Although it is wide, the street's relatively unbroken skyline and serious atmosphere make it feel like an urban canyon.

A second important new street was Marshalsea Road, built to link Great Dover Street with Southwark Bridge Road. It too was built by the MBW and opened in 1888. Blackfriars Bridge was also replaced. As early as 1832 it had been noticed that the bridge was in a poor state of repair, but it was not until 1869 that its replacement was opened. This new bridge was widened in 1910.

Some of the most striking structures in Bankside are the viaducts that carry the railways from London Bridge to Charing Cross or Cannon Street and from Elephant & Castle to Blackfriars. These massive pieces of civil engineering were built in the early 1860s and while they assisted the railway companies, its commuting passengers and the overall development of London's economy, for the residents of Bankside (and some of the businesses) they were a disaster. On a local level they caused as much destruction and disruption as the two fires of the 17th century or bomb damage during World War II.

The South Eastern Railway's lines that had previously ended at London Bridge were extended to Charing Cross in 1862-64 and to Cannon Street in 1866. Not to be outdone, the London, Chatham and Dover Railway (L,C&D) in 1864 extended its line from Elephant & Castle to Blackfriars. In 1878 a link was made between the South Eastern and the L,C&D's lines where they cross near Blackfriars Road. These new lines were carried on massive brick viaducts. They traversed an intensely urban area and many properties were demolished to make way for them. The railway companies clearly wished to minimise their costs and so where possible routed their new lines over residential rather than industrial areas. This approach gave them two advantages: residential land values were lower than industrial ones and few residents, most of whom were extremely poor, had the resources or capacity to challenge the railway companies' actions.

Bankside also briefly had its own railway stations. From June 1864 onwards, before the L,C&D extended to the City, it had a terminus just east of Blackfriars Bridge. This continued in use as a through station until 1885. The South Eastern also had a station between London Bridge and Waterloo at Blackfriars Road. The station was in operation from 1864 until 1869, when it was superseded by the new station at Waterloo (now Waterloo East). More enduring were goods yards. The L,C&D's station became a goods yard and the South Eastern operated a very large concern called the Grand Vitesse Depot near the site of its short-lived station. The Grand Vitesse depot continued in use until 1966.

THE SPREAD OF HOUSING

The building of new roads in the early 19th century accelerated development in Christ Church parish and St George's Fields. A series of new institutions established themselves in St George's Fields, as discussed in Chapter 3; houses were built along Blackfriars Road and other main roads.

The northern part of Christ Church parish developed rapidly after the building of Blackfriars Bridge and the laying out of Great Surrey Street. Many of the houses on the main roads were of good quality and imposing size: they included those on Blackfriars Road (built 1765-90); the eastern portion of Stamford Street (c.1790); and Nelson Square (c.1807). New streets were laid out, such as the western sections of Stamford Street (1803 and 1815) or the smaller streets east of Blackfriars Road such as Pitt Street (now Scoresby Street), George Street, Charles Street, Edward Street, William Street (now Gambia Street) and Robert Street. New houses were built on existing roads such as in Bear Lane and Green Walk (now Burrell Street).

In contrast, the first buildings on St George's Fields were houses of the lowest quality. They were built by members of the Hedger family, who ran the "Dog and Duck" tavern on land leased from the Bridge House Estate; although the tavern had gained a poor reputation and created a nuisance, the Bridge House Estate was prepared to lease the Hedgers more land for development. From the mid-1780s onwards, James Hedger obtained leases of most of the Bridge House Estate land in St George's Fields and started a programme of housebuilding. In doing this, he was acting at the edge of the law: he took control of much of the land before the leases had been signed, the building activity was against the wishes of the City, who did not wish to see their land built on, and in spirit it went against the fields' status in most people's minds as a common.

Unfortunately, once Hedger had a legal tenancy the City was powerless to stop him. The City authorities had hoped to prosecute Hedger for building on common land, but as the land was for the common use only of those who owned or leased it (as opposed to the population at large) and because Hedger had a controlling interest in virtually all of the land, they realised that their case would fail and so took no action. Consequently, during the 1790s the Bridge House Estate witnessed the erection of buildings of the lowest quality inhabited by the poorest of tenants.

Above: The sign of the Dog and Duck Tavern and the Bridge House Estate. The Bridge House Estate uses the cross of St George (also known as the Southwark Cross) to identify the buildings it owns in the area. The City took exception to the cross being incorporated into the Southwark Borough Coat of Arms in 1900, despite the fact it commemorates one of the borough's ancient parishes. This sign is in the collection at the Cuming Museum.

Hedger also irritated St Saviour's parish by building a retail market on St George's Fields. The parish objected as they feared the market would challenge Borough Market, but their fears were unfounded as Hedger's enterprise proved to be small. The market stood in the triangle between Borough Road, London Road and Newington Causeway. It enjoyed an advantageous location, was outside turnpike charges and had plenty of stabling for horses. Initially it was a food market, but after the 1870s it dealt in furniture and household goods. In 1902 the site was sold to the London County Council.

In the late 18th century other landowners, prompted by the improved transport connections and resulting higher land values, also started to build on their land. The Temple-West family, who owned about two acres of land in St George's Fields, built houses in West Square, St George's Road, Temple Place, Blackfriars Road and Belvedere Place to the north of Borough Road. The houses in West Square were the most substantial and were occupied from 1794 onwards; in the early years of the 19th century West Square was home to the wealthy and influential. Various members of the Hedger family lived there until the 1820s, Robert Barker, a painter of panoramas, lived there until his death in 1806 and Henry Perkins, a partner in the large and profitable Anchor Brewery on Bankside, lived there in 1848-49. Some of the buildings mentioned above remain today as the most substantial domestic properties in north Southwark.

In James Smith's words of 1813:
> "St George's Fields are fields no more,
> The trowel supersedes the plough;
> Swamps huge and inundate of yore,
> Are changed to civic villas now."

The Southwark Local Studies Library has a large collection of deeds from the Temple-West estate and its management can be traced from the construction of the first buildings through the 19th and 20th centuries. Throughout the early 1790s the West family let land in small plots for periods of around 90 years to a variety of developers. These developers, variously described as "stationers", "surveyors" or "ironmongers", then built houses, which they sub-let to tenants. Typically, each developer built only a small numbers of houses; the largest number mentioned is 50. At the expiry of the head lease the houses came back into the direct control of the Temple-West family and consequently there is a further large batch of leases dating from the later years of the 19th century.

While most of the Temple-West estate was of undeniable quality, its surroundings were uninspiring. On one side were the shabby tenements built by James Hedger, and on the other was land that remained undrained. This meant that surface water could only run away in open ditches, and with the building of many new houses these ditches started to serve as foul sewers. Passing vehicles turned the surface of the land into a quagmire in wet weather.

The Bridge House Estate was well aware of the potential value of its land and the fact that it was being undermined by Hedger's actions. Consequently, in the early years of the 19th century it set out to retrieve the situation by draining the area and taking action against Hedger's developments. Draining was first suggested in 1807, when the City, along with neighbouring landowners, promoted a bill on the subject in Parliament. The bill was passed two years later, but no action was taken for a further ten years. In 1810 a second Act was passed, which abolished all common rights and so allowed landowners a much freer hand in building. Also in 1810 many of Hedger's leases expired and the City decided not to renew them. This development clearly displeased Hedger, who proceeded to destroy many of the buildings he had built in an attempt to salvage the materials. Hedger probably saved the City a job as many of the houses were of such poor quality they would have been demolished anyway. The City furthermore refused to maintain any of the houses that remained.

The City drew up a number of grand plans for the development of the fields, but very few of their schemes were ever built. The one exception to this was around St George's Circus, where buildings with a concave frontage were erected at an even distance from the centre of the junction. The concave front of the "Duke of Clarence" public house still survives. The rest of the Bridge House Estate land was let to developers (but not the Hedgers) on building leases; land owned by other bodies was similarly dealt with. The Bridge House Estate still owns a good deal of property in the area and its mark appears on many of these buildings. It also gave its name to a pub, the "Bridge House", on Borough Road. Many of these building plots followed the shape of the original medieval fields and this explains the unusual pattern and orientation of some of the streets in the area today: Lancaster Street, Boyfield Street (previously Gun Street) and Rushworth Street (previously Green Street), which all run obliquely to the surrounding streets, are good examples.

The City briefly and optimistically hoped to see St George's Fields develop as a well built, respectable and desirable suburb, but they must have been greatly disappointed in the result. Far from being home to the "civic villas" of which James Smith wrote, St George's Fields was by the last half of the 19th century one of the worst slums in London. The rapid downturn was an inevitable consequence of the area's proximity to London and in particular the increasing industrialisation of the riverside district to the north and west. The prospect of jobs drew in a new population, but much of the work was unskilled and casual; workers needed to live near their (potential) places of employment. The area was fully built-up by the middle years of the 19th century and the most recently developed streets were mean and poorly built. The houses on the grid of streets between Webber Row and Borough Road and the courts between Southwark Bridge Road and Great Suffolk Street were particularly small. The problem of overcrowding was made worse in the later 19th century as space further north, which previously had been used for housing, was increasingly used for industry or railways.

The lack of proper drainage or refuse collection compounded the area's difficulties. Such problems were common to many other places, but were made much worse in Southwark by the density of the population and the fact that water courses did not naturally flow towards the river – much of the area was below high water, so the contents of the foul sewer flowed backwards during incoming tides. The consequences of these conditions are discussed in Chapter 3. The recurrent threat of floods from the River Thames led the St Saviour's Board of Works to take action to improve flood defences in the late 1870s.

BANKSIDE AT WORK

In the late 19th century an observer noted that there were a greater variety of trades and manufacturers in Southwark than in any other district in the kingdom. London's role in trade and finance is of course widely recognised, but its place as a centre of manufacturing industry deserves greater recognition. Southwark, and particularly Bankside, were well placed for industry: close to the river, so allowing for the easy delivery of raw materials, convenient for the main market in London and containing high-density housing for workers in the labour-intensive trades. The extent and variety of trades and industries grew consistently through the 18th, 19th and early 20th centuries. No buildings, however sacred or distinguished, were safe from the industrialising process: by the early 19th century, even the great hall of the Bishop of Winchester's palace was in industrial use — as a mustard factory.

WHARVES AND WHAREHOUSES

The River Thames was London's main artery of trade in medieval days and while valuable goods were offloaded at the legal quays on the north bank of the Pool of London, more general goods, such as foodstuffs, were landed in Southwark. Bankside lies upstream of London Bridge and so tended to be served by lighters, which unloaded their goods at the many riverside wharves and inland warehouses. Wharves were a feature of Bankside from Roman Times, while large-scale warehouses in which goods were stored became prominent in the 18th century. These high, brick buildings made an austere narrow canyon of the streets beside the river, while cranes occupied the space between the warehouses and the river wall, removing goods from lighters. The process was very labour-intensive and the river provided a great deal of employment, much of it unskilled and casual in nature.

St Mary Overy's Wharf was built by George Dunnage for a Mr Doo in 1882 and was used first as a granary. Its lifting gear was powered by hydraulics from the London Hydraulic Power

Company. This could well have been from the Falcon Wharf Pumping Station, built in the same year, just to the east of Blackfriars Bridge. (The Falcon Wharf Pumping Station was re-equipped in 1906 but ceased operation in 1935, reverting to use as a warehouse). In later years, many other types of goods were stored, for instance in 1885 Egyptian beans and sugar. Cole and Carey, who also had warehouse premises in nearby Mill Street, took over in 1885 and used the building to store rubber, varnish, tinned goods and, after World War II, dried fruit. In 1948 the proprietors of Hay's Wharf (Tooley Street) acquired the premises.

Rosings' and Stave Wharves were due south of St Mary Overy's and west of Southwark Cathedral. Over the years hops, sugar, seeds, corn, butter, bacon, cheese, rubber and canned goods were stored in them.

BREWING, VINEGAR AND HOPS

Southwark's position as an important centre of the brewing industry was noted in Chapter 1. In its early days, brewing was a local craft industry – each ale house brewed its own ale for immediate consumption. Hops, introduced to England from the Netherlands, gave beer its bitter taste and acted as a preservative.

From the 17th century onwards, and particularly after the Industrial Revolution, wholesale breweries grew up to supply a chain of ale or public houses. The most famous of these Bankside breweries, indeed at one time the largest brewery in London, was the Anchor Brewery. Its history goes back to the mid-17th century, when James Monger, "Citizen and Clothworker of London", opened a brewhouse close to the site of the Globe Theatre. Ownership then passed to James Child, a liveryman of the Grocer's Company who, in 1670, practised "the art and mistery of brewing". Towards the end of the century, an enterprising young man by the name of Edmund Halsey took a job as broom clerk that involved no more than sweeping up the premises; within two years he had married the boss's daughter and in 1693 took over the business.

Halsey was an astute businessman and the brewery thrived under his direction. He also had political ambitions, but in 1710 was accused of bribery and so prevented from taking his seat as MP for Southwark. In 1719 he was made Governor of St Thomas's Hospital; he was elected MP for Southwark in 1722 and again in 1727. He had no son to carry on the business and so his nephew Ralph Thrale was brought in, who, in the words of Dr Samuel Johnson, "was employed for 30 years at 6 shillings a week in the brewhouse that was afterwards his own". And he paid for it as well, for Halsey's will directed that "all my stock in trade shall be sold for the best price that can reasonably be gotten". The price was £30,000 – an indication of the brewery's growth, for 100 years before it had changed hands for just £400.

Ralph Thrale was an enterprising man, MP for Southwark, High Sheriff of Surrey and Master of the Brewers' Company. He amassed a fortune, enabling him to educate his son, Henry, at Oxford; Johnson remarked of Henry that "although in affluent circumstances, he had the good sense enough to carry on his father's trade". Henry Thrale inherited the business in 1758 and soon married Hester Lynch Salusbury, who was talented, quick-witted and possessed a lively mind much interested in the arts. Johnson was a firm friend of the family. In 1773 a special beefsteak dinner was served at the brewery in the company of Johnson, Sir Joshua Reynolds, Oliver Goldsmith, David Garrick and Edmund Burke – Mrs Thrale was enthralled by Johnson and his circle. Johnson had his own room set aside at the brewhouse and even advised on its running. During a period of financial difficulty, he wrote to Mrs Thrale that "the first consequence of our late trouble ought to be an endeavour to brew at a cheaper cost ... unless this can be done, nothing can help us."

Meanwhile the day-to-day running of the brewery was left to its long-suffering manager, John Perkins. Perkins' moment of glory came in June 1780: while the Thrales were away taking the waters in Bath, the brewery became the target of mob violence. Thrale, following in the family tradition as MP for Southwark, had shown sympathy for Roman Catholic emancipation and this motivated the Gordon rioters to seek reprisal. Fresh from their assault on Newgate Prison the mob surged south of the river.

They were met at the brewery gate by Perkins, who, according to Boswell, bought them off with "fifty pounds worth of meat and porter". They returned, of course, but by this time Perkins had called in the troops. He was hero of the hour!

Henry Thrale was soon to die and Hester determined, with Johnson's help, to sell up. "For Sale" signs were stuck on the brewery walls and noticed by David Barclay (of Barclay's Bank fame) while he was out walking. "This will do for young Robert" he exclaimed, speaking of his American-born nephew. The day of the sale was fixed for 31 May 1781. Johnson, as executor to Thrale's will, was "bustling about, with an ink horn and pen in his button hole, like an excise man, and on being asked what he really considered to be the value of the property answered "we are not here to sell a parcel of boilers and vats but the potentiality of growing rich beyond the dreams of avarice". Mrs Thrale was well pleased to get £135,000, exclaiming "God Almighty sent us a knot of rich Quakers who bought the whole." The Barclays were astute enough to take John Perkins in with them with a quarter share and the brewery became known as The Anchor Brewery, changing to Barclay, Perkins and Co in 1791.

Barclay Perkins' Anchory Brewery. The most productive brewery in London in the 19th century. A view of 1841 from The Penny Magazine.

Around this time the "horse wheel" that was used to raise water from the brewery's well was replaced by a Boulton and Watt steam engine. It was installed by William Murdock, generally recognised as the founder of the gas industry, but at the time working for Boulton and Watt. Barclay wanted some indication as to how the work done by the new steam engine compared with the horses he was using at present. Murdock came up with the definition of one horse power as 33,000 feet pounds per minute, an engineering definition, born in Bankside, that was to last until the days of decimalisation.

Barclay, Perkins and Co went from strength to strength. There were many famous and indeed infamous visitors in the 19th century. One such was the brutal Austrian General Haynau, notorious for his flogging of women; the draymen did not take kindly to his reputation, chasing him off the premises and a mob joined the hunt, forcing the general to take refuge in a dustbin. There were demands for a formal apology but Foreign Secretary Lord Palmerston took the draymen's side, much to the dismay of Queen Victoria. The incident so thrilled the Italian Patriot Garibaldi that he asked to see the brewery where "the men flogged Haynau" on his visit to London in 1864.

Other Bankside breweries were the "Peacock", in existence in the mid-18th century on a site just off Gravel Lane (modern Great Guildford Street) and the "Old Barge House Brewery" on the site of the Royal Barge House at the east end of Upper Ground.

Supporting the brewing industry in Southwark and elsewhere in London was the hop trade. Bankside and in particular Borough High Street was the centre of London's hop trade. Even the old letter-based telephone code was HOP. The dried hops were transported from Kent, either to London Bridge Station or via the river, in "pockets", for storage in one of the many warehouses in the area. Pockets were large round bales of hops, about 6 feet in length by 2 feet in width (180 centimetres by 60 centimetres) and weighed about one and a half hundred weight. A one pound sample was taken from the pocket, marked with the producer's name or code and laid out with other samples on a special board in the hop factor's well-lit showroom for inspection by merchants.

There were two groups of middle men – the factors were agents for the producers, while the merchants acted for the brewers.

Hop picking began at the end of August. A large force of casual labour was needed and thousands of Londoners took their annual holiday in the hop fields of Kent. It is engaging to think that for the people of Bankside this would often be something of a bus man's holiday, for these very folk could well have worked at one of London's largest breweries – Bankside's Barclay, Perkins and Co.

The hop trade thrived in the 19th century, so much so that a group of City speculators built a Hop and Malt Exchange in Southwark Street. It opened in 1867 with the intention of providing the hop growers, merchants and dealers with a single market centre. The exchange hall measured 80 feet by 50 feet (24 metres by 15 metres) and was surrounded by offices on four floors with ornamental galleries embellished with hop seed designs overlooking the trading floor. Something of a white elephant, it was never used for its original purpose. Now converted to offices, it was recently happily restored by English Heritage and is a wonderful building and a real gem in Southwark Street. Note in particular the central pediment to Southwark Street that depicts lively scenes of the hop industry.

There were many firms of hop traders in the area including Wood, Hanbury, Bevan, Jackson & Co in Borough High Street and Wigan Richardson of Southwark Street. The latter firm commissioned the construction of a large warehouse at 61 Southwark Street with a capacity of 10,000 pockets. It soon acquired other warehouses at Calvert's Buildings, 15 Southwark Street, opposite the Hop Exchange.

Malt vinegar is a natural offshoot of brewing and the works of Robert and Arthur Pott moved from Whitechapel to Bankside in 1790. They had their works on the site bounded by Sumner Street, Great Guildford Street and Southwark Bridge Road. It was one of the largest vinegar works in the country.

POWER: GAS, ELECTRICITY AND WATER

Bankside Gas Works was opened in 1814. The works were just west of Pike Gardens and on the site of the later power station. They had one gas holder, a retort house, various sheds, office accommodation and a house for the manager. In 1828 it was taken over by the Phoenix Gas, Light and Coke Company and became known as the Phoenix Gas Works.

The Phoenix was in bitter competition with its rival, the South Metropolitan Gas Company, set up in the Old Kent Road in 1833. The competition led to chaos in the streets of South London, with both companies laying pipes in the same street and competing for business from the same householders. At one time the Phoenix was selling its product at 9 shillings per 1000 cubic feet, undercutting South Metropolitan's price of 11 shillings for the same quantity. "The purity and illuminating power of our gas is such that 3000 cubic feet will burn as long and give as great a light as 5000 cubic feet of the gas of the Phoenix" retorted the South Met. But the Phoenix won the day and the Old Kent Road company was forced to reduce its prices.

Eventually the two companies merged, with the South Metropolitan taking over the Phoenix in 1880. Gas manufacture at Bankside continued until just before World War II, at which time the plant was dismantled and effort concentrated at the Old Kent Road plant. Our only visual reminder of the gas industry in Bankside today is a stained glass memorial window directly over the altar in the retrochoir (Lady Chapel) in Southwark Cathedral. It is dedicated to 386 employees of the South Metropolitan Gas Company who lost their lives in World War I.

Electricity was supplied from Bankside to power Londoners' homes for 90 years. The first Bankside Power Station began generation on 12 June 1891. By today's standards it was tiny. There were two pairs of 25KW arc lighters and two 100KW alternators. They were belt-driven and powered by steam from Babcock and Wilcox boilers. But expansion was rapid – within the year new engine rooms and boiler houses were built and with the addition of further machinery, capacity rose to 10,500KW. The station was now the largest establishment of its kind in the world.

At about this time Bankside began to provide power to the newspaper industry in Fleet Street. Previously the newspaper owners had generated their own power and they insisted that Bankside should provide security of supply – "for the papers must come out on time". Supply was direct current and steam was supplied by somewhat dated marine boilers because the owners did not wish "to risk their supply depending on new-fangled boilers of the water tube variety".

In the early days of operation it was difficult to cater for rapidly changing demands for power. London fogs were an ever-present headache. Within a few minutes of the onset of a London "pea souper" demand for power could rise dramatically, and then equally quickly fall again when the fog lifted. The company tried to get knowledge beforehand of the coming of fogs by arranging for notice of them to be phoned through from the docks to the east – it was reasoned that fogs came from this direction. However, messages tended to arrive after the fogs had lifted and this instigated a policy of having a look out posted high up on an observation platform around one of the chimneys.

The Post Office also had its own electricity-generating station at the west end of Upper Ground.

A further example of Bankside providing power to London was the London Hydraulic Power Company (LHPC). Using water pumped under pressure through a network of 6-inch (15-centimetre) pipes, the LHPC powered many lifts, jacks, presses, cranes and hoists in docks and railway yards throughout London. It had a double association with Bankside. It had its main offices on Hatfields and the first of its five pumping stations was in the area, just east of Blackfriars Bridge. The company was in operation from 1883 to 1977.

FOOD

The food industry was also a major feature of Bankside life.
While in the medieval period the produce from fields and fish
farms mainly supplied the local population, in the 18th and 19th
centuries Bankside provided for a much wider market. The first
way it did this was as an area for market gardening: examples of
market gardens were the asparagus garden in Christ Church
parish run by Mr Bovey and an orchard on the site of Nelson
Square. The name of the "Jolly Gardners" pub, which stood until
recently at the corner of Union Street and Great Guildford Street,
is another reference to this activity.

From 1890, near Blackfriars Bridge was the warehouse and
factory of the well known food retailer, J.Sainsbury. The
company's original warehouse was in Kentish Town but by the
end of the 1880s expansion had dictated newer and more
extensive premises. Cox's Horse Repository in Stamford Street,
the supplier of Queen Victoria's first riding horse, came up for
sale. There was a clause in the lease restricting use to a horse
repository but Sainsbury overcame this and furthermore obtained
the site at a knock-down price, so beginning an association with
Southwark that continued until very recently. Their shop on
Stamford Street opened in 1894. Sainsbury recognised the value
of the area (and Bankside in general) to the food industry. It was
near to the centre of overseas food importation at Hay's Wharf in
Tooley Street, close to Smithfield Market and had good rail links.

Pascalls was a well known firm of confectioners, founded in 1866
by James Pascall, son of a Croydon baker of Huguenot descent, in
a small, two-roomed shop just off Oxford Street. Starting with
"Surprise Sugar Eggs" and herbal cough drops, expansion was
rapid and a move to much larger premises at Valentine Place,
Blackfriars Road, was celebrated with the introduction of a range
of new products including barley sugar and almond rock. James
Pascall was a kindly man. He was one of the first employers to
pay his workers during Bank Holidays as well as during their
annual summer holidays. He was involved in charitable work,

supplying repaired second-hand shoes to London's needy. Governor of Borough Polytechnic, magistrate and member of the London School Board, he was also concerned with the welfare of mentally handicapped children. Early in the 20th century a new factory was acquired at Mitcham and the two factories ran side by side until Blackfriars Road was destroyed in World War II. In 1959, the company became part of the Beechams Group, makers of the famous Murray Mints.

Members of the animal kingdom were also catered for in Bankside. "Sherley's Foods And Medicines For Dogs and Cats" had premises at 18 Marshalsea Road; their brochure stated that some items contained a small percentage of an ingredient mentioned in the Poisons Act but was quite harmless if used in accordance with the instructions on the packet. One such was "Sherley's Aphrodisties" – "a cure for impotence in dogs and cats and invaluable for shy breeders", price 1 shilling 6d, postage 1d.

Two fine buildings associated with the provisions industry still stand on Valentine Place. No 1 was built in 1812 for Charles James Percival, a food dealer, and was rebuilt in 1882. At the junction with Webber Street is a graceful yellow-brick building with elaborate stone window surrounds. This was built in c.1910 as new premises for the Maltina Bakery Co.

J.T.Davenport Ltd of 83-87 Union Street manufactured the famous Victorian remedy for coughs and stomach upsets first invented by Dr J. Collis Browne. After his remedy was successful in 1854 in controlling a cholera outbreak in Durham, Collis Browne went into partnership with J.T.Davenport and began manufacture in Union Street. The infamous brew contained an extract of opium and chloroform and certainly worked, but its contents were later to prove its downfall. By the 1970s, considerable business was being done with high-street chemists for the medicine to be sold over the counter but new regulations restricted its opiate content to much lower levels, so much so that it ceased to be effective. That was the end of J.T.Davenport Ltd – a single product company!

There were many other food producers in Southwark: Epps Cocoa manufacturers were on land previously occupied by the Falcon Glass Works and James Ashby, a packing company for tea and coffee, were in Union Street – as much as Tooley Street, the whole area could justifiably be called "London's Larder".

ENGINEERING

Many celebrated engineers have been associated with Bankside, none more so than the members of the Rennie family. In 1784 John Rennie, who had been trained at Edinburgh University, was put in charge of installing a new Boulton and Watt steam engine at Albion Flour Mills, just east of Blackfriars Bridge. In 1791 he set up a business of his own in nearby Stamford Street. His first interest was canals and he was involved with fen drainage, but he is best known for dock and bridge building. Apart from his docks in London he worked at Hull and Liverpool. He designed the first Southwark Bridge as well as the first Waterloo Bridge, described by Venetian sculptor Antonio Canova as the "noblest bridge in the world, worth a visit from the remotest corners of the Earth" – praise indeed! The business was continued by John Rennie's sons and it was John (later Sir John Rennie) who completed his father's London Bridge in 1831. As well as building stationary and marine engines, the firm also constructed a number of railway locomotives. In the 1850s they opened a shipyard at Deptford Creek.

The engine Rennie installed at Samuel Wyat's Albion Flour Mills made the mills the talk of London. Using the engine, 20 pairs of millstones were able to grind ten bushels of wheat every hour of the day and night – far greater productivity than was possible with traditional water and wind power. Many millers lost their livelihood. The mills even became a tourist attraction and were visited by Thomas Jefferson, at that time American ambassador to France. Open for just three years, the Mills were destroyed by an enormous fire on the night of 3 March 1791. Some say the fire was caused by arson – indeed, millers were that night seen dancing for joy on Blackfriars Bridge. The *Star* newspaper reported that "millers within 30 or 40 miles of London have been in a state of intoxication since Wednesday last." Rennie and Wyat, however, believed the fire started accidentally and was caused by the friction of badly lubricated machinery. A popular song of the day sums up:

> *"And now the folks begin to chat,*
> *How the owners did this and that.*
> *But very few did sorrow show,*
> *That the Albion Mills were burnt so low."*

David Kirkaldy was another Bankside engineer with an international reputation. Like Rennie he was a Scot, born in Dundee in 1820. His early working life was at Robert Napier's Vulcan Foundry in Glasgow, but in 1861 he set out on his own to design a machine to test construction materials placed under stresses such as pulling, thrusting, bending, twisting, shearing, punching and bulging. Greenwood and Batley of Leeds built his testing machine and this was soon installed at the Grove in Southwark, next door to the engineering firm of Easton and Amos. Southwark Street was soon to be cut through and it was here at No 99 that Kirkaldy moved in 1874. The works were sold in 1965 but the original machine is still in place at the Kirkaldy Testing Museum, set up in 1983 at 99 Southwark Street. It typically applied a load of 300 tons and was used to test materials for the new Blackfriars Bridge and from the Tay Bridge after its failure in 1879.

James Easton came to the Grove early in the 19th century and soon went into partnership with Charles Amos. In 1844 they built the waterworks for the newly opened Trafalgar Square. The firm was a well-known manufacturer of beam engines and exhibited at the 1851 Great Exhibition. One of their beam engines, now preserved at The Kew Bridge Steam Museum, worked for 80 years at a pumping station in Northampton. Another, now housed at the Westonzoyland Pumping Station Museum near Bridgwater, performed sterling work over many years draining the Somerset Levels.

The Dog and Pot, the sign of Hayward's the ironmongers of Blackfriars Road. This postcard was part of a campaign to save the sign, which is now in the Cuming Museum.

Edward Hayward, senior partner in the Union Street firm of Hayward Brothers, in 1871 invented and patented a revolutionary system for illuminating basements. The patent, entitled "Improvement in Pavement Lighting", employed a clever use of optics, not only to allow light to pass through the glass-covered pavement but also to direct it in an inclined direction to the basement below. This was done with a series of glass prisms beneath the pavement light, so arranged as to direct the incident light in the required direction. In addition to pavement lights, the firm made a number of other products, such as coal hole covers (many of which remain in Blackfriars Road), iron staircases and collapsible steel gates for lifts. Before establishing themselves in Union Street, Hayward Brothers had been at "The Sign of the Dog's Head in the Pot" in Blackfriars Road.

James Adams was another inventive man. One day in 1882 he was lying in bed with a painful attack of sciatica and feeling even worse because his bedroom door had not been shut properly, resulting in a continual rattling. The noise so got on his nerves that he determined to do something about it. Thus was born his pneumatic door spring hinge or slave, patented in 1890 as "Improvements in and in connection with door closing apparatus". The firm of James Adams and Son started in Union Street but later moved to 26 Blackfriars Road.

The 19th century saw an enormous expansion of industry in South London, reflecting London's vast population increase and its need to be supplied with goods. In 1890 the booklet *South London Illustrated* was published and in it are detailed scores of small concerns operating in the Bankside area. There were manufacturers of dyes, hot water radiators, disinfectants, chemicals, scales and weighing machines, boots and shoes, sacks and tarpaulins, photographic dark rooms, black lead, dust bins and surgical instruments to name just a few, as well as umpteen foundries and general engineering works.

FURS AND HATS

One of the more unusual industries, and one for which the area was famed, were fur cutters, which supplied hat manufacturers. Sennett Brothers were in Holland Street, as were the premises of Mr H.Kent at No 43. At Kent's – who styled himself "Henry Lee's Successor" after the firm's founder – rabbit skins were imported from Australia and New Zealand (home stock apparently being in short supply). From the warehouse the skins would progress to the "pulling rooms" where armies of women plucked out the coarse upper hair to leave the pelt with fur alone. Then it was to the "carroters" who brushed the fur with a solution of quicksilver (mercury) and nitric acid to give it a silky texture. (It is easy to see where Lewis Carroll's "Mad Hatter" originated because mercury is now known to be highly toxic and its effect on the poor girls of Southwark would have been severe.) After drying, the pelts were cut to size ready for the market, both at home and abroad. One of Kent's customers would have been Frederick Upton, Hat manufacturer and Hosier, whose shop was on the corner of London Road and St George's Road. Upton made extravagant claims for his silk hats, going so far as to suggest that "if to your share some trifling worries fall, wear but these hats and you'll forget them all".

Hats had been made in north Southwark since Tudor times, because the felt was a by-product of the tanning industry. One of Bankside's hat manufacturers designed the first bowler hat. In 1850, William

Coke of Holkham Hall, Norfolk, asked his London hatter, Lock, to create a new shape of hat because his top hat kept blowing off in the wind and was damaged by rain or brambles when he went riding. Lock passed the problem to one of its suppliers, Thomas Bowler of Southwark Bridge Road, who developed the famous shape of the bowler hat, and also found a way to harden the felt. This versatile hat made Bowler's fortune; in the 1860s he went into partnership with Victor Jay. By the 1930s Jay Hats were employing 600 people, but the factory was bombed in World War II and never reopened.

The largest hatmakers in Bankside were Tress and Co. Their head office is now the "Mad Hatter Hotel" in Stamford Street. The business was started in 1846 by Cooper Tress, making top hats. He expanded the firm, diversifying into ladies' hats, pith helmets and cloth caps. In 1873 he was able to build his head office and then bought a large house in Clapham. Cooper Tress died in 1903 and one of his sons, Sidney, ran the business until his death in 1953. At that time the firm was sold to Christys of Bermondsey, who closed the Bankside factory and transferred the work to their premises in Bermondsey Street.

PRINTING

There has long been a fine tradition of printing in Bankside. As long ago as 1529 Peter Treveris, described as "this ingenious and elegant printer", printed his "Grete Herball".

Pioneer lithographic printers were Max and Co of Borough Road, who claimed to be the first to use steam to power their presses and Barclay and Fry of Southwark Street, who printed cheques and business stationery. One printer who became very well known was Robert Bowers, who had a factory in Blackfriars Road. He served on the Christ Church Vestry, was a Guardian of the Poor, a governor of Morley College and a Progressive Liberal in politics. He also wrote a history of the area, *Sketches of Southwark Old and New*. Fine printing was carried out by Loxley Brothers of Southwark Bridge Road and printing presses were made by Robert Hoe of Borough Road.

Burrups were an old established firm, opening as Burrup, Mathieson and Sprague at 114 Southwark Street at the turn of the 19th century. They had started "At the Sign of the Crane" in the City in 1628 and began the custom of using the endpapers of their books to advertise other titles. John and William Burrup were keen followers of cricket. Associated with Surrey Cricket Club at the nearby Oval it was William who took the first English touring side to Australia in 1861, years before Test Matches or The Ashes were thought of. Burrups' reputation rested on their work for the City of London. They had an advert each morning at the top lefthand corner of the *Financial Times,* promising "Speed, Accuracy and Security".

STREET TRADERS

Many members of Bankside's population worked not for established industries but for themselves. Costermongers, who sold fruit and vegetables or fish from a handcart in street markets or on the road, featured strongly in the population. The costermongers worked from home – few would want to have lived above or next to the ones who dealt in smoked fish, as the smoking was usually carried out in the ground floor of their home. Other foul-smelling trades included bone boiling, bone grinding and cat-gut making. The annual report of St Alphege's Church, Rushworth Street, for 1883 vividly describes the sources of local employment: "the population consists of 'costers', bricklayers and other labourers, porters, dock labourers, coal heavers, dustmen, hawkers, wood choppers, match-box makers, beggars, thieves, prostitutes and a miscellaneous remainder who get their living in unknown ways."

Except for The Cut, which was well known for cheap clothes and food, there were no major shopping streets in the area. For larger shops people had to travel to the Elephant & Castle or Lower Marsh. The busiest shopping times were Friday and Saturday nights and Sunday mornings.

LOCAL GOVERNMENT:
SHIFTING RESPONSIBILITY

In the 18th and 19th centuries arrangements for the government of London were complicated, but even by the standards of the day the circumstances in Bankside were particularly confusing. In the 18th and early 19th centuries, the typical pattern of government in London was for the parishes, or vestries, to have responsibility for most aspects of local administration, while the county dealt with wider matters through the court of quarter session, which was overseen by justices of the peace. What we think of today as capital projects, such as the building of roads, were dealt with by local Acts of Parliament. The parishes were responsible for things such as the poor law, the watch and local roads.

The general pattern was applied locally in Bankside – the three parishes of St Saviour, which covered the eastern portion of the riverfront, Christ Church, which covered the western portion and St George the Martyr, which covered the inland area of St George's Fields. Reforms were made at the local level in 1856 when vestries were reformed and some were superseded by Boards of Works and thereafter given increasing responsibilities. In 1900 these bodies, and various Boards and Commissions that had been established for specific purposes, were superseded by the Metropolitan Boroughs. In 1834 and again in 1869 the poor law was reformed and responsibility was taken from the parishes and given to newly-formed Boards of Guardians.

At a wider level the county's powers were challenged in 1856 by the creation of a new body with London-wide responsibilities. This was the Metropolitan Board of Works (MBW), which had responsibility for building London's main sewer system and for main roads. In 1889 the MBW was superseded by the London County Council (LCC) and at that time Surrey's role in the administration of Southwark ended. The London School Board, which was responsible for municipal education, was established in 1870. Its duties were passed to the LCC in 1904.

But in Bankside the pattern was additionally complicated by other factors. Firstly, the City of London had rights of administration that conflicted and overlapped with those of the county – the "Dog and Duck" tavern appealed to Surrey after the City refused to renew its licence in 1787. Secondly, a particularly large number of Boards and Commissions were established, exercising powers that had been removed from the parishes. Paving commissioners were established to pave, light, clean and watch the streets in various districts: from 1786 onwards, the Clink Paving Commissioners performed this function in the area of the ancient Clink manor; others included the Holland Street Paving Commissioners (from 1793 onwards), the Christ Church Paving Commissioners (from 1811 onwards) and the Upper Ground Paving Commissioners (from 1819 onwards). The Clink Paving Commissioners, for example, erected numerous bollards, some made from redundant cannons, to keep encroaching vehicles off footways – and many of these remain in place today.

Thirdly, an unusually high proportion of responsibilities remained with the ancient vestries after the creation of Boards of Works in 1856. For example the Corporation of Wardens of St Saviour (as that vestry was properly known) continued to administer the parochial charities. Fourthly, there was another spate of creating Boards and Commissions for specific purposes in the 19th century: a St Saviour's Burial Board from 1852; Baths Commissioners for St George the Martyr from 1876 and for St Saviour's from 1892; and Library Commissioners for St Saviour's from 1892 and for St George from 1895. Finally, none of the reforms (including those that set up the Metropolitan, or for that matter London Boroughs) ever extinguished the ancient manorial courts, which still exist for minor matters.

In the mid-1890s there was an attempt to make the northern part of Southwark part of the City of London. The idea was proposed by the Southwark parishes themselves and had the support of the City Corporation, but was vigorously opposed by the LCC, which stood to lose powers in the area, and by Southwark's neighbouring parishes. The proposal failed but it made a useful contribution to the wider debate about London's government that resulted in 1900 in the abolition of the vestries and the formation of the Metropolitan Boroughs. Locally the inefficient tangle of administrative arrangements was brought to an end and the Metropolitan Borough of Southwark was established, receiving virtually all the powers and liabilities of the vestries, the Board of Works and the various Boards abolished at that time.

A visible legacy of the parish arrangements are the boundary marks that survive in some places. There is a decrepit stone marking the boundary of Christ Church and Lambeth in Pontypool Place, off Valentine Place; high on a building on Southwark Bridge Road near its junction with Marshalsea Road are two marks next to each other for the separate parishes of St Saviour and St George the Martyr.

CHAPTER 3

Bankside 1750-1914:
People and society

The process of industrialisation and urban development
described in Chapter 2 was accompanied by huge social changes
in the area. This chapter examines these changes and the
social fabric that bound the area's population. It falls into two
broad sections, examining firstly the institutions and charities
established on St George's Fields in the period after 1750,
and secondly the social problems caused by the intense
urbanisation of the later 19th century.

THE CHARITIES AND
INSTITUTIONS OF ST GEORGE'S FIELDS

In the late 18th and early 19th centuries a number of ground-
breaking charitable institutions moved to St George's Fields. The
area was recently developed with new roads, it had fresh air and
(initially) clean water, there was space to build and expand, and
it was free of the hustle and bustle, and vice, of London. These
institutions were distinct from parochial charities as they had a
London-wide or even wider remit and often provided care of a
type not seen before.

BETHLEM HOSPITAL

The largest of the institutions in St George's Fields was the
Bethlem Hospital. This was an ancient institution, originally
established in the City, to care for the mentally infirm. Its name
was corrupted to "bedlam", now a universally used term for
uproar and chaos. By the late 18th century its premises at
Moorfields were unsuitable, and the hospital began to look for a

new location. St George's Fields was ideal for the reasons detailed above and also because it offered the hospital a home on land owned by its parent organisation, the City of London. The hospital took the lease of a plot of land in the southeastern corner of the fields on the site of the former "Dog and Duck" tavern.

The new building was designed by James Lewis, the hospital's surveyor, and opened in August 1815. It was in an austere classical style with long wings to the east and west and had space for 200 patients. In an attempt to improve hygiene (but not the comfort of the patients) the windows of the wards were initially unglazed. The building cost £122,000, provided mainly in the form of government grants. The hospital took on a new role after its move to Southwark, when it agreed to a government suggestion to hold criminal lunatics. By the 1830s the cells and wards were overcrowded and so two new wings were added to the rear of the building; the north front was modified when Lambeth Road was realigned. The dome was added in 1844-45. (The present dome is a replica built after a fire in 1968.) In the mid-1850s the inmates' windows were glazed and furnishings improved, reflecting a more compassionate treatment of patients.

In the later 19th century the hospital increasingly took private, paying patients, who were often of genteel origin. The mentally ill poor were cared for by newly built county asylums and in 1864 criminally insane inmates were transferred to Broadmoor Hospital. Among Bethlem's inmates were the painter Richard Dadd, who had murdered his father, and Louis Wain the artist famous for humorous and sentimental paintings of cats. By the late 19th century, the hospital's focus was on giving humane and progressive care to private and often well-off patients. However, its buildings and its location were no longer suitable: the building was designed for a more austere age, and the area had become poor, unhealthy and overcrowded. In 1930 the hospital moved to new purpose-built accommodation at Monks Orchard in Beckenham, Kent. The building it left was later converted into the Imperial War Museum.

MAGDALEN HOSPITAL
AND OTHER INSTITUTIONS

Although the Bethlem Hospital was the largest of the institutions to move to St George's Fields, it was not the first. The Magdalen Hospital for Penitent Prostitutes, established in 1758 by Robert Dingley and Jonas Hanway with the aim of reforming and retraining prostitutes, had moved to a site on the west side of Blackfriars Road, just north of St George's Circus, in 1772 from its previous home in Whitechapel. The hospital flourished in its early years, benefiting from a good location some distance from the vice of central London and from the fact that it was the only body in London carrying out such work. It was largely financed from collections made at public services at its chapel, and this arrangement provided a good income: in the hospital's early years, attendance at its services was popular in certain well-off sections of society. One of the Magdalen's most popular preachers was Dr William Dodd, later hanged for forgery in 1777. The hospital was unusual in two respects: although highly moral in its aims and methods, it was not a religious foundation; and unlike many charities, which had land or investments from which they could gather income, it depended entirely on donations. Curiously, although the hospital's records provide details about its staff, funds and premises, they say very little about the number of women it worked with, exactly how it helped them or how effective its work was.

As the 19th century progressed, the hospital became dissatisfied with its site: the area was poor and overcrowded and the vice from which it was trying to remove the women was openly taking place in the immediate vicinity. The Magdalen was additionally hampered because other chapels had been built in the area, breaking its monopoly on donations from wealthy worshippers. In 1869 the hospital moved to Streatham.

A near-neighbour of the Magdalen Hospital was the Philanthropic Society, a charity for the care of children involved in crime or having criminal parents. The society was founded in 1788 in Hackney and moved to St George's Fields, on a site near London Road, in 1793; like the Magdalen Hospital, it received income

Above top: St George's Circus showing the obelisk, the School for the Indigent Blind and in the background the Bethlem Hospital along Lambeth Road. A watercolour of 1839 by Sidney Shepherd.

Top: The Freemasons' School, Westminster Bridge Road. A print of 1803.

from collections made during services at its chapel. Boys were taught manual trades and girls domestic service. As the character of St George's Fields changed during the 19th century, the Philanthropic Society suffered a similar fate to the Magdalen: falling income and a location now too close to the vices and temptations from which the society had hoped to remove those in its care forced it to depart. It moved to Redhill in 1848.

The School for the Indigent Blind was a secular institution that took people from all over London and provided an entirely new form of care. The school was established in 1799, initially using space in the "Dog and Duck" tavern and later, after 1810, in purpose-built premises at the junction of Lambeth Road and London Road. The school raised income through donations and through selling goods produced in its workshops. Its work was less affected by the change in character of St George's Fields, but it too was forced to leave in 1901 when the Bakerloo Line Underground railway compulsorily purchased its site for a railway depot.

Other new institutions established in the area were more exclusive. The Royal Freemasons' School for Girls was established in 1788 and was located on the north side of Westminster Bridge Road. It provided schooling for 100 girls aged up to 15 years, the daughters of freemasons. Like other institutions, it left the area as the character of St George's Fields dropped, moving to Wandsworth in 1852. There were also two sets of almshouses for members of City Livery Companies. The Fishmongers' Company almshouse was established in 1618 at the corner of St George's Road and Newington Butts; another member of the company founded an adjacent almshouse in 1719. Both moved to Wandsworth in 1851. In 1820 the Drapers' Company built almshouses in Glasshill Street. Although now used for other purposes, these still stand.

A new addition to the parochial charities was Hopton's Almshouses, which were built in 1752. The almshouses were founded after the death of Charles Hopton in 1731. Curiously he never lived in Southwark, but he did own land in Christ Church parish. The almshouse provided home for 26 poor people. Hopton's Almshouses, which still stand in Hopton Street, are unusually large for a private benefaction.

Many other individuals also left buildings or investments, the proceeds from which were to go to charitable causes. John Stock's charity, founded in 1780, gave clothing to poor women; Christopher Ridout's gave food to the poor and William Boyce, in 1816, left money for an organist to play the instrument he erected in Christ Church. In 1895 the parochial charities were amalgamated and administered by the Corporation of Wardens of St Saviour.

BANKSIDE'S SOCIAL PROBLEMS

From the mid-19th century onwards, an increasing proportion of Bankside's population lived in conditions that 150 years later we would judge to be obscenely overcrowded and unhealthy. The following section discusses the extent of the problem, how it had come about, attitudes to the problem, the gradual efforts at reform and their results. While many of the processes described here are part of the story of London or even of national history, they are worthy of attention as Bankside provides examples of the problems at their most acute and the area featured in the process of improvement.

RISING POPULATION

Bankside's population grew significantly after 1750, peaked in the late 19th century and declined thereafter. Putting some detail on the bald outline presents problems as this book's definition of Bankside does not follow administrative boundaries and because the pattern of population change was not uniform across the whole area. The main source of population figures is census returns, which were collected for the whole country every ten years from 1801 onwards. In 1801 the totals for the three Bankside parishes were – Christ Church: 9,933; St Saviour: 15,596; and St George the Martyr: 22,293; a total of 47,822. If we take it that about one half of St George's parish is outside the scope of this book, then the total for our area for 1801 is about 36,000.

By 1831 this figure had reached about 52,000 and in 1861 (when the riverside parishes of Christ Church and St Saviour reached their peak population), 63,000. The total population for the area fell after 1861 and in 1901 it was about 52,000. In 1861 Christ Church had a population density of 220 persons to the acre and St Saviour nearly 150 to the acre – in comparison that figure today is about 60 to the acre. The riverside parishes' population fell by one-third between 1861 and 1901. On the other hand, St George the Martyr's population peaked in 1901, when its population density reached 213 persons to the acre.

This overall rise in population was sustained by massive immigration: without this the population would have declined in a very short time. London's death rate exceeded its birth rate until about 1800 and its death rate was in excess of that of the country as a whole until roughly the same date – it would seem that people came to London to die! Despite these unfavourable conditions, Bankside's population trebled over the period 1750-1861. People came to the area from many parts of Britain. Most came from surroundings counties – Surrey, Kent, Sussex and Essex – but the Celtic fringes also contributed many. A large Welsh community settled in the later 19th century, and monopolised the dairy trade. There were also many Irish. Many of these were forced from Ireland during the famine of the 1840s and settled in St George's Fields. They, and their descendants, made up perhaps 10 per cent of the population.

The riverside area's population fell in the last third of the 19th century as land previously given over to housing was increasingly put to industrial and commercial uses. These new uses fell broadly into two categories: manufacturing industry and new railway lines and roads.

As discussed in Chapter 2, the railway companies built new extensions, carried on brick viaducts, into central London. As part of the process they were required to count the number of people made homeless to make way for them, but there was no incentive to do so accurately and so significant under-recording must certainly have taken place. Thus the London Bridge to Charing Cross extension officially displaced 4,580 people and the London, Chatham & Dover's extensions to Farringdon and Victoria, 3,150 (perhaps one-third of that figure was within Bankside). The

London Bridge to Cannon Street extension officially displaced only 557 people and the building of the junction of the Charing Cross line with the line from the Elephant & Castle to Blackfriars displaced 2,118. "Displaced" meant that the people were made homeless; the railway companies had no duty to re-house those involved. The laying out of Southwark Street in 1864 made about 4,000 people homeless.

Consequently the population in the affected areas fell significantly. Christ Church parish's population fell from 17,000 to 14,500 between 1861 and 1871. In the same period the population of St Saviour's parish fell from 19,000 to 15,600. Despite these falls, it is likely that the population density stayed much the same as the proportion of land available for housing fell dramatically. At the same time the quality of housing fell: the wealthier moved away but the poor could not do so – they were unable to pay the higher rents of farther afield, they needed to remain to be close to possible places of work and they knew that moving from the area would have removed their qualification to claim poor relief. Consequently they stayed, living in more cramped accommodation that was also more expensive than before because there was less space. Instead of clearing slums – as the vestries had hoped – the construction of the new railway lines made the slums worse.

HOUSING

In the mid-19th century, the housing stock in the area fell into three broad categories: very old houses in the riverside area; larger ones built at the end of the 18th century and in the early 19th century on the main roads and in St George's Fields, originally aimed at middle-class tenants; and a huge number of increasingly poorly built slums. During the late 18th and early 19th centuries, the Blackfriars Road district was a prestigious one. Among its residents were the engineers, the Rennies, in Stamford Street and the poet Percy Shelley and Thomas Barnes, editor of *The Times,* in Nelson Square.

As the area's population increased, particularly from 1850 onwards, so housing conditions deteriorated, especially in St George's Fields.

Sumner Street, 1895.

Those that moved in were poor, looking for casual work. The change encouraged the wealthy to abandon the area, especially as they could travel to work on horse buses and trams. Virtually everybody rented their home; ordinary families rented at best half a house or more commonly a room. On average people could expect to spend about one-quarter of their income on accommodation. As landlords found that most profits were to be gained from wealthier tenants and very little from the poor, there was a downward spiral of poorer tenants providing landlords with no incentive to maintain properties, resulting in even poorer properties that could only be let to those even further down the poverty scale. People, usually men, of the poorest means stayed in common lodging houses, which provided only the most meagre of shelter.

As is shown above, population densities were correspondingly appallingly high. The effect of this at individual house level was, after 1856, an average for the parish of St George of seven people living in each dwelling house with instances of 20 people per house being common. The most densely occupied areas were near Zoar Street, to the north of Southwark Street; Bear Lane to the south of Southwark Street; between Union Street and Orange

Street (now Copperfield Street); the area between Southwark Bridge Road and Great Suffolk Street (known as "the Grottos") and a large area east of Blackfriars Road between Friar (now Webber) Street and Borough Road. Contemporary accounts of these conditions were vivid. A report compiled by St Alphege's parish in 1883 described the conditions in which its parishioners lived. Of the area to the west of Southwark Bridge Road it said:

> "here the costermongers, tramps and thieves dwell, in close, ill-built, pestilential courts, in filth, squalor and degradation. Their little homes are so closely huddled together that scarcely three feet of yard space is left at the back ... Bold coarse-faced, slatternly women gossip or quarrel at the doorsteps; ragged, peaked-faced, hungry-eyed children fight in the gutters; the loose blaspheming riffraff of the thief world hangs round the public-house door, or staggers noisily through the streets."

UNSANITARY CONDITIONS

The other huge problem facing the area was that of public health. The starkest evidence for the extent of the problem is to be found in death rates that were consistently above the London average. For the second half of the 19th century the death rate per year in the St Saviour's area hovered around 25 per 1,000 population, in St George the Martyr it fluctuated between 25 and 30 per 1,000 and in its worst district, Borough Road, was often above 30 per 1,000. Levels of infant mortality were also particularly high. In St Saviour's area in 1860 it was calculated that 50 per cent of the population did not reach the age of five years and even by the 1890s 20 per cent of children died before the age of one year.

The principal threats to public health were overcrowding, chronic disease, careless disposal of human waste and a polluted water supply. Until the early 19th century, the River Thames was sufficiently clean to be a reasonable source for drinking water and much of Southwark's water supply came from commercial waterworks on Bankside. However, the Thames at Bankside and elsewhere in inner-London was used as a direct source of drinking water long after the river had become appallingly polluted. This pollution was a major contributory factor in the outbreak of cholera in 1849 (when 5 per cent of the Bankside population died) and again in 1853 (when 4 per cent of its population died). Drinking water was usually dispensed to the public from a shared standpipe or pump and the supply was discontinuous and non-existent on Sundays. Residents usually stored water in outside water butts but these were unprotected and frequently stagnant or contaminated.

The cause of the contamination of the River Thames was its use as an open sewer following the invention of the flush toilet. Before this time human waste was disposed of as so-called night-soil, which was carried from dry cesspits to be deposited on nearby fields. In the 18th century St George's Fields was a suitable location for such activity, being large, close to London, undeveloped and of poor soil quality. Contemporary street names make reference to this process – Vine Yard, just off Marshalsea Road, was previously called Harrow Dunghill. However this activity declined after the 1780s when the area started to be built up. Flush toilets overloaded existing sewers, which previously were only there to carry surface water away. Because it was low-lying the St George's Fields area was especially disadvantaged by this unpalatable cycle. Even after 1819, when the City of London made proper arrangements for the drainage of the area, the sewers only took waste away for eight hours each day during the falling tide; at the highest tides there was a wash of river water (and all it contained) back towards, and sometimes into, low-lying buildings.

Cholera was not the only disease to concern the Medical Officers of Health; other potent killers were smallpox, tuberculosis and typhus. A typhus outbreak in 1864 in St George the Martyr's parish had the highest mortality rate of anywhere in London.

The disposal of human remains was also an issue for public health, as by the 1850s parish and other burial grounds had become full to overflowing. Bodies were buried in extremely shallow graves and there were frequent references in parish reports to noxious gases escaping from the churchyards.

POVERTY

While all agreed that the area was poor, any objective assessment of just how poor is difficult as there were no agreed criteria as to what constituted poverty. But Bankside's residents certainly were poor relative to their peers elsewhere in London, and this fact was acknowledged. In 1856 in his first ever report as Medical Officer of Health of the parish of St George the Martyr, William Rendle (also an important writer on Southwark's history) explained the problem thus:

> *"we are a most melancholy parish, low in level and low in circumstances. The lowest and poorest of the human race drop from higher and richer parishes into our courts and alleys, and the liquid filth of higher places necessarily finds its way down to us. We receive the refuse as well as the outcomings of more happily situated places."*

Charles Booth's poverty survey map 1889. Booth surveyed London's streets and classified its residents by their relative wealth or poverty. Reds and pinks indicate relative affluence while blue meant "very poor, casual, chronic want" and black, "lowest class, vicious and semi-criminal". Note also the large area given over to industry, which is shaded blue / grey.

The first thorough comparative survey of poverty was not done until 1889 when Charles Booth classified London's streets by the relative wealth of their residents. Of the area near Stamford Street, Booth said: "The inhabitants make one vast, poor family whose lives are well known to one another. There is more street life than even in the East End, more children in the street and more women gossiping at the doors." Of the area just north of Borough Road, he said it had "the reputation of being as poor and rough as any place in the [police] division".

OFFICIAL INACTION

The attitudes of those in power locally to these problems was consistent with the approach of central government. In the first instance many were, and wished to remain, ignorant of the problem. But even if there was an understanding of the problems of public health and a consensus as to the remedies, there was little political will to make the necessary changes.

In general the authorities – local or national – agreed that they had no responsibility in matters of public health. Set against the appalling conditions prevalent, we would see this view as callously complacent, but in fact those in authority really were powerless to effect change. In the first instance, the causes of poor health and disease were not understood – even something so straightforward as the relationship between polluted drinking water and illness was not established until 1849. Equally, no systematic investigation had been taken of the living conditions of the poor. (Arguably Charles Dickens, through the living conditions graphically described in his novels and journalism, brought the state of Victorian London to people's notice more than any government report.) After 1856, when the vestries were reformed and each vestry or Board of Works had to hear an annual report from its Medical Officer of Health, the availability of information improved. The reports often made uncomfortable reading, both for what they reported and the criticisms made by the Medical Officer of Health about the vestrymen's lack of activity in dealing with the problem. There was a particularly combative relationship between William Rendle and the vestrymen of St George the Martyr. In frustration at lack of action from the vestry, Rendle said of his political masters: "low rates rather than low mortality are made the test of public prosperity" and resigned his position.

The vestries did not in truth have the resources to offer much support. National government dismissed health issues as local problems and the vestries could only spend the money they raised from rates gathered in their area. Thus poor areas with the greatest problems had less to spend than wealthy areas with fewer difficulties. The parish saw its role as providing assistance only to the most destitute and did all it could to limit expenditure on the poor.

REFORM

IMPROVING HOUSING

The provision of housing was unregulated until the mid-19th century. Only in the second half of the 19th century were vestries given powers to order landlords to make improvements or, in extreme cases, give orders for demolition. Even then the vestries were often unwilling to intervene in this way for practical and principled reasons. They objected in practice as doing so was usually counterproductive because improved properties commanded a higher rent than the poor could pay, and demolition, a power they had from 1868, simply displaced the problem by making the existing tenant homeless. They objected in principle because they did not agree that it was their role to intervene and because intervention could mean incurring expenditure they did not wish to make.

In the 1860s so-called "model dwellings companies" – bodies intent on providing higher-quality high-density housing in purpose-built tenement blocks – appeared. These organisations were popularly called "5 per cent philanthropists", because they required this level of return on their investments and made it by

Peabody Buildings, Blackfriars Road, 1872. From the Illustrated London News.

charging higher rents and through imposing very strict tenancy rules. A good, and early, example of the work of one of these bodies is Cromwell Buildings at the north end of Red Cross Way. Cromwell Buildings were erected in 1864 by the Improved Industrial Dwellings Co. The Peabody Trust did similar work, but because its money came directly from its benefactor, George Peabody, it called for a smaller return on its investment and so rents were lower and its work was able to benefit more people. A Peabody estate was built in 1870-71 on Blackfriars Road on the site of the Magdalen Hospital. This was the first Peabody estate in south London. Its building was warmly greeted by the authorities and they commented approvingly on the better health of its residents. A second Peabody estate was built on the north side of Southwark Street on the site of part of Potts' Vinegar Works. Another notably large example of model dwellings was Queen's Buildings in Scovell Road, which was built in 1881 by the National Model Dwellings Co on the site of the King's Bench Prison.

Although we may see the model dwellings of the late 19th century as barrack-like, they were significantly better than the housing they replaced. Their density was high, but they had good facilities, were designed for single-family occupancy, were let at a fair rent and were run by professional management. However, they sadly benefited only a small minority of people in the area as the companies had very few sites – they only obtained them at slum demolition, which yielded only small areas, or when commercial sites came available, which was expensive. Additionally, only a minority of people in the area could meet their higher rents and more stringent letting conditions.

If these housing societies had their idealism overwhelmed by circumstances, a far more remarkable example of idealism and determination was shown by Octavia Hill, who was responsible for the housing built on land owned by the Church of England, later the Church Commissioners, in north Southwark. Before her time the housing that had been built on this land by private landlords was generally of a very poor quality, so when the leases on these sites expired Octavia Hill had the properties pulled down and replaced by cottage-type buildings in a rustic style. She also operated a stricter regime of repairs and management. There are many examples of her work in the area, for instance Red Cross Cottages on Red Cross Way and, immediately behind them, White Cross Cottages on Ayers Street built in 1890; Winchester Cottages on Copperfield Street of 1894 and Whitehill Houses on Sawyer Street are other examples.

Widespread significant change did not come until the work of the London County Council in the very late 19th century. The LCC had greater powers of demolition, funds with which to build new homes and the ability to manage housing itself. Some of the LCC's intervention was demolition-only, such as Grotto Place (so called after Finch's Grotto, the 18th-century pleasure ground) off Southwark Bridge road. The LCC provided flats at Merrow and Ripley Buildings in Kings Bench Street (1896-97), Albury and Clandon Buildings in Gun (now Boyfield) Street, three large blocks on the north side of Borough Road (1900), and five blocks in Webber Row, off Waterloo Road (1905). Together the model dwelling companies, Octavia Hill and the LCC started to break the hold of irresponsible private landlords and, for those that could afford their rents, their new developments provided a higher standard of housing than hitherto.

POOR RELIEF

The solutions to poverty and ill health developed only slowly. During the 18th and 19th centuries public authorities provided only the most basic level of social assistance to the poor. Each parish ran a system of poor relief, which was given as money, clothes, food or coal, work and through the workhouse. As the 19th century progressed, the authorities increasingly also provided care to the sick – for the sick were poor and the poor, sick.

The parish funded the assistance from local taxes based on the value of residents' property: rates. It was not until the later 19th century that they received funding additional to monies raised locally. As many of the parishes were poor to start with, the amount that could be raised to support the poor was small and the modest number of wealthier rate payers resented supporting what they sometimes saw as a population of largely undeserving paupers. There was therefore a double incentive to control the amount spent on poor relief and the parish authorities did all they could to limit the liabilities they faced. Paupers applying for relief were examined as to their place of origin and if they proved not to be from the local parish were required to return from whence they came; mothers of illegitimate children claiming relief were required to name the father, who was pursued to pay towards the cost of the child's upbringing. Pauper children were apprenticed, often en masse, to employers a long way from home and, most notoriously, the workhouse – the place of last resort for the destitute – was made as uninviting and uncomfortable as possible in an attempt to keep to a very minimum those calling on its services.

The Christ Church parish workhouse was in Marlborough Street, on the western boundary of the parish. The St Saviour workhouse, which was rebuilt in the 18th century, was on a site behind Winchester House, Southwark Bridge Road, later part of the fire station site. St George's workhouse was in Mint Street. There were pauper burial grounds at Winchester House and in Union Street near its junction with Red Cross Way. The latter burial ground was also known as the Cross Bones burial ground due to supposed (but untrue) associations with the medieval Bankside prostitutes.

In 1834 and again in 1869 the administration of the poor law was reformed and responsibility was taken from the parishes and given to the newly constituted Boards of Guardians. Until 1869 there were two Boards of Guardians in the area: St Saviour's, covering St Saviour and Christ Church parishes, and St George the Martyr. St Saviour took control of the whole area in 1869 and in 1901 its name changed to the Southwark Union.

THE BEGINNINGS OF HEALTHCARE

There were no public hospitals in London until infirmaries, run by the poor law authorities, developed as separate institutions after 1867. Before this date the sick were cared for by private doctors, at the ancient hospitals such as St Thomas's or Guy's or at privately run charitable institutions. In the late 18th and early 19th centuries a number of private institutions were established at St George's Fields and their work is described earlier in this chapter. The Boards started to tackle many of the fundamental healthcare problems. From 1877 onwards, there was a dedicated infirmary for the area at Newington and this provision was improved by the building of a new infirmary at Champion Hill, Dulwich, in 1887. The Boards of Guardians also set up temporary hospitals during outbreaks of disease, such as by St George's during the typhus outbreak of 1864. A major contribution was in the provision of vaccinations for smallpox from 1871 onwards. The Boards also ran other forms of social care, notably special schools at Hanwell and Mitcham for orphans or abandoned children.

In addition, there were other hospitals of a more specialised nature providing care to a wider population. The Evelina Children's Hospital, on Southwark Bridge Road, was established in 1869 by Baron de Rothschild, whose wife, Evelina, died in childbirth. It closed in 1975. The South London Opthalmic Hospital was founded at St George's Circus in 1857 to provide care to those with diseases of the eye. It expanded and changed its name to the Royal Eye Hospital in 1886. It closed in 1980. The Royal South London·Dispensary, opposite the Bethlem Hospital, provided diagnosis and medicines to the sick from 1841 onwards.

CLEANER WATER, BETTER HYGIENE

The solution to the problems of water supply and sewage disposal are very much part of London-wide history. The Medical Officers of Health noticed the differing death rates between the customers of the two companies that supplied the area. The residents of St Saviour's parish, customers of the Southwark and Vauxhall Company, which took its water from polluted Battersea – this company had absorbed and closed the waterworks on Bankside in 1834 – died five times more rapidly than those in neighbouring Christ Church, who were supplied by the Lambeth Company, which took its supply from cleaner Thames Ditton. The report that established these facts was influential in convincing the authorities that cholera was waterborne. The Southwark and Vauxhall Company moved its supply to Hampton in 1855 and many of the problems were solved.

Southwark Street at its junction with Borough High Street, 1865 - one year after its opening. Note the ornate sewer vent pipe, the costermonger's cart and how the traffic has expanded to fill the new road space.

The problem of sewage disposal was solved by one of the biggest civil engineering projects in London's history: the building by the Metropolitan Board of Works of a system of main sewers that carried sewage and rain water to outfall stations east of the capital. When Southwark Street was laid out an important part of this network was built beneath it and an ornate vent pipe near its junction with Borough High Street gave a visual and olfactory clue to its presence

By 1857 the churchyards and crypts of the three old Anglican churches were closed and, as there was no alternative municipal provision, thereafter residents of the area had to find a place to bury members of their family as best they could.

Public baths, for washing the person and clothes, have their origin in attempts to improve public health. The first public baths in the district opened in Lavington Street in 1893. It provided two swimming pools, private baths and a laundry and by 1900 it was receiving about 500,000 visits per year.

Amongst the mass of people and industry, it was almost impossible for the authorities to find any open space that could be used for recreation. Their achievements were limited to using the closed churchyards and the centre of the two large squares in the area, Nelson Square and West Square. When the Grottos, an area of slum housing near Southwark Bridge Road, was pulled down its site was also used as open space. Otherwise residents had to travel to Kennington or to Southwark Park in Rotherhithe.

SOCIAL CARE: SETTLEMENTS, HOMES AND CHARITIES

Charities were established in the later 19th century to help with some of the area's social problems. The most important and long-lasting of these was the Blackfriars Settlement in Nelson Square. Settlements were bodies that carried out social and community work in deprived parts of London and other cities. They had their origins either in religious denominations, or more commonly in educational establishments, typically public schools or universities. Members of the school or university with a social conscience, often prompted by a religious or political conviction, and the drive to apply themselves to some practical work settled in a deprived area and undertook programmes of social relief.

There were numerous settlements of this type in London and Southwark: local examples include Cambridge House, in Camberwell; Charterhouse in Southwark and the Oxford & Bermondsey Club. Blackfriars Settlement was established in 1887 as the Women's University Settlement in the poorer districts of London. Initially its members came from the Universities of Oxford and Cambridge, but the University of London participated from 1892 onwards. Its aim was to provide social welfare, especially for women and children, and to foster "schemes to elevate them physically, intellectually and morally". The settlement recruited from university students, who were trained in various aspects of social work and then became resident for a year or more. Work with disabled children was a special priority in the early days; many of the children were suffering from tuberculosis. The children were offered training in trades, and a shop was established to sell the goods they made. There was a school, which included provision for disabled children, and a children's holiday fund. The Acland School was a type of youth club, with outings, classes, social evenings and performances. The settlement's income came from subscriptions, residents' payments and visitors' payments. Prominent in the settlement's activities was a Miss M.A.Sewell, who was represented on its committee from the very early 1900s through to the late 1930s. The settlement was greatly assisted by its early acquisition of three houses, Nos 44-46 Nelson Square.

Other organisations appeared in the mid- and late 19th century to provide care for more specific groups. Prominent amongst these were Sharman's Homes in West Square and Fegan's Homes in Southwark Street. Both were children's homes, founded by individuals with a deep religious conviction who gave their name to the body they established.

Charlotte Sharman started her work with orphans from the Southwark area in 1862, when she started to make arrangements for them to be cared for by families in the country. In 1867 she established her orphanage in a house in West Square and soon afterwards she was caring for 42 children, with capacity for 80 in total. She later expanded into two houses, using one as an Infants' Home and the other for the care of sick children. Her approach was unusual not in its provision for orphaned children – the poor law guardians and other charities did similar work – but because the care she offered was available to all and did not feed into the system of child labour. The orphanage provided accommodation under the care of a matron and had its own school (not to be confused with the London School Board School that now carries her name). She also acted as an adoption agency. In 1875 she started to build a purpose-built home in Austral (then South) Street on the site of one of the first houses she had occupied. This was finally finished in 1884. The Homes were funded from donations and subscriptions; it was estimated in 1868 that it cost £15 per year to care for each child. Idealistic and deeply compassionate to the needs of the poor, she was also very level-headed and ran the financial side of the homes prudently, guided by a single and frequently stated rule – no debt. Under Charlotte Sharman's vigorous and determined guidance – she described herself as obstinate – the organisation expanded and later ran homes in Stockwell, Tunbridge Wells and Hastings.

Another important children's home in the area was Fegan's Home in Southwark Street. Fegan's did not originate in Southwark, and had a shorter time in the area, but provided a home and education for many of the area's boys during the time it was there. Fegan's Homes were started by J.W.C.Fegan in 1872 in Deptford; he opened his premises on Southwark Street in 1882. He remained in the area until 1913, when the Southwark Street lease ran out and he moved to Westminster. His work in the field, like that of Charlotte Sharman, was prompted by a deep religious conviction, in his case the result of a spontaneous religious conversion in 1870.

EDUCATION

SCHOOLS

Educational provision in the mid-18th century was limited to that provided by St Saviour's Grammar School, parish schools, or private education at home or in small private academies. The 18th century was generally a low period for grammar schools such as St Saviour's, so most sons and daughters of middle-class parents were educated privately. By the early 19th century, St Saviour's School was in a poor state. The 1818 Parliamentary enquiry into grammar schools showed that the number of pupils had fallen greatly, rarely more than 40 and sometimes as low as 25, when the school's capacity was 100. There was also an impression that the parents of wealthier residents were not sending their sons to the school and reports of lax discipline among staff and pupils. After this investigation, and criticism by the parish, matters improved, with tighter discipline and a larger roll. The improvement was brief, as the enlargement of Borough Market in the late 1830s forced the school to move to smaller and poorly situated premises in Sumner Street. The number of pupils continued to decline, as did income.

Set against St Saviour's decline – which was not unusual for an ancient grammar school – St Olave's had been expanding, moving to successively larger premises. In 1896 St Olave's suggested that the two schools should merge. St Olave's were keen for this to happen as St Saviour's was by then in receipt of funds from a revised scheme of management for Dulwich College (to pay for Dulwich College's commitment to educate boys from St Saviour, the home parish of Dulwich College's founder, Edward Alleyn). St Olave's wished to use some of St Saviour's resources towards its plan to expand and found a girls' grammar school. The merger took place and a site was found for the new girls' school in the New Kent Road. The school opened in 1903.

St Saviour's was not the only ancient endowed school with a royal charter to have its home in the Bankside area. From 1830 to 1922 King Edward's School occupied a site between the Bethlem Hospital and West Square. The school was founded in 1553 in the

City of London, one of a large number of schools whose foundation is associated with this monarch and which have taken his name. It had a complex origin in King Edward VI's gift of Bridewell Palace to the City in 1553 for use as a place for the reception of poor, homeless children and for the punishment of offenders. A medieval palace, part prison and part school, was an unsuitable location for teaching and in 1830 the school moved to a new site in St George's Fields. In 1850 the foundation's role became exclusively educational. The school provided a general and industrial education for boys and girls up to the age of 18 years. The emphasis was on educating boys for the Royal Navy and girls for work in domestic service. The boys' school moved to Witley in Surrey in 1867, and the St George's Fields site was used for the girls' school until it closed in 1922.

Educational provision for the population at large grew as the 19th century progressed. It was dominated by two societies: the National Society, which was affiliated to the Church of England; and the British and Foreign School Society, which was affiliated to the Nonconformist churches. The activities of both expanded, especially after 1833 when they started to receive a state subsidy. In addition, so-called "Ragged schools", whose income was derived entirely from charity, provided for the very poor.

The National Society came to control the three parochial schools, St Saviour's, Christ Church and St George the Martyr. St Saviour's School was established in 1704 and was entirely separate from the grammar school. From 1808 onwards it shared premises with the Newcomen Schools, another charity foundation, in premises in Union Street. (The building it occupied in Union Street from 1908 onwards still stands.) This arrangement did not last and the boys part of the Newcomen School later occupied premises in Southwark Bridge Road before they moved to Newcomen Street in 1864. The St Saviour's parochial school has evolved into the modern Cathedral School in Red Cross Way. The Christ Church school was founded as a parochial charity in 1713 to provide schooling for up to 20 boys from the parish and provision was made to include girls from 1719. It became part of the National Society in 1836. The St George the Martyr school was established in 1698 and occupied premises on Borough Road in 1839-1901 and on Thomas Doyle Street thereafter.

The Joseph Lancaster monitorial system in action. From Manual of the system of primary instruction, pursued in the Model Schools of the British and Foreign School Society, *1837.*

The British and Foreign School Society had its origin in the pioneering work of Joseph Lancaster, who ran a school in Borough Road from 1804. Lancaster introduced the so-called monitorial system of teaching, whereby older pupils, called monitors, taught younger pupils in simple and rigidly planned lessons – in this way, large numbers of pupils could be taught by a single member of staff. Lancaster claimed that up to 700 pupils were receiving lessons at Borough Road in 1804. In 1814 the Royal Lancastrian Society, founded by Lancaster to carry out his work, became the British and Foreign School Society. Initially Lancaster's methods of teaching were widely influential both in England and overseas, but because of the narrow curriculum and mechanical learning they became increasingly unpopular as the century progressed. However, they provided mass education to some of the poorest children in London. The society used the premises in Borough Road as its national headquarters and for teacher training. The premises were rebuilt in 1817 and enlarged in 1842 and were used until 1888, when the society and the teacher training college moved to Isleworth.

There were also Roman Catholic Schools in the area. The first to be established, and the only secondary school in the area today, is

Notre Dame Girls' School, adjacent to St George's Cathedral. This was established in 1855 by the sisters of Notre Dame from Namur in Belgium. A boys' school was set up shortly thereafter and the Church of the Most Precious Blood ran a school shortly after its establishment in 1892.

The single biggest change in educational provision was the establishment of the London School Board (LSB) in 1870. This was charged with providing schooling for all children aged 3-13 years. It was estimated that should all children have wanted to attend school there were only places for about 75 per cent of them. The LSB started a vigorous campaign of school-building and by 1884 had erected seven school buildings, including West Square (1884, now Charlotte Sharman School and the only one of the new LSB buildings still used for the purpose for which it was built), Webber Row and Orange Street (which stand but are used for other purposes) and three others, now demolished. Together these schools provided places for 5,000 children.

Attendance at London School Board schools was compulsory, although the truancy officer was as cautious as the police in venturing into some of the rougher alleys and courts to put his case; schooling was free after 1891. The authorities approved of the LSB's provision and its higher standards, but grumbled at the extra cost it put on their rates. They were right to comment that the LSB's schools were supplanting as opposed to supplementing existing provision, and many of the church schools contracted or closed altogether. After 1904 responsibility for education passed to the LCC and this body started to make provision to send children on to secondary school.

HIGHER EDUCATION AND BOROUGH POLYTECHNIC

Bankside briefly boasted its own learned institute. This was the Rotunda, later the Surrey Institution, which stood on the west side of Blackfriars Road, very close to the bridge. It was founded in 1788 as a museum to house a natural history collection that included objects collected by Captain Cook. As the name suggests, the Rotunda was a circular structure, built in a classical style.

This venture was a financial failure and the building, then renamed the Surrey Institution, was used for lectures on the sciences and other related subjects. These too had a limited audience and the building was later used for entertainments, plays, concerts and meetings.

Today South Bank University dominates much of the area around Borough Road and St George's Circus. The University has its origins in the Borough Polytechnic Institute, which was founded in 1892 to promote "the industrial skill, general knowledge, health, and well-being of young men and women belonging to the poorer classes". This was one of a number of polytechnics founded in London in the later 19th century to provide technical, vocational and recreational education to the masses. Borough Polytechnic occupied the premises on Borough Road vacated by the British and Foreign School Society in 1888.

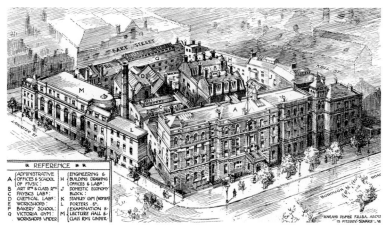

Borough Polytechnic. A view of from The Borough Polytechnic Institute, its origins and development, *by Edric Bayley.*

The polytechnic was funded by charitable and state funds and was governed by a body that included nominees from the London School Board and the LCC. From 1904 onwards, it enjoyed an increasingly close relationship with the LCC. By 1909 more than 3,800 students had enrolled for its classes. The polytechnics related their technical education to the trades operating in the areas in which they were located; consequently classes were run in tanning, typesetting, printing, metalwork, and chemical and electrical engineering. All were heavily subscribed. The polytechnic's teaching emphasis was on industrial utility and classes were aimed at students who had been through only elementary school. The majority of the polytechnic's work was in the form of evening classes and the teaching staff were mainly part-timers with a trade, as opposed to an academic, background. The polytechnic expanded almost from the date of its foundation, prompted by high demand for its classes and new sources of funding.

Morley College, in Westminster Bridge Road and just across the border in Lambeth, was founded at the same time as the Polytechnic. It shared the polytechnic's aim of educating the local population, and complemented the polytechnic's curriculum by providing classes in the arts, literature and music.

PUBLIC LIBRARIES

Three public libraries opened in the area, in Southwark Bridge Road in 1894, Borough Road in 1898 and Blackfriars Road also in 1898. The Borough Road Library was assisted by a grant of £5,000 from the philanthropist Passmore Edwards. By 1900 they were together receiving about one million visits each year.

PUBLIC SAFETY: THE FIRE BRIGADE

Prominent on Southwark Bridge Road and occupying the whole block between Sawyer Street and Copperfield Street is Winchester House and other buildings occupied by the fire service. From 1878 to 1937 this was the headquarters of the Metropolitan Fire Brigade, and today houses their main training centre and a museum.
The Metropolitan Fire Brigade (MFB) was established in 1865 after the great fire of Tooley Street of 1861 disastrously showed that previous arrangements, based on private insurance companies, were inadequate. The MFB was placed under the control of the Metropolitan Board of Works. Before they moved to Southwark Bridge Road there was a fire station at 97 Southwark Street. The Southwark Bridge Road site had three main components: a fire

station built in 1878 (which still stands there); the main headquarters building, which was used as such until 1937 when this function moved to the Lambeth Embankment (this building was damaged during World War II and pulled down in 1969); and Winchester House, which was originally built as a large private home in 1820 and was used as the residence of the Chief Fire Officer until 1938. The most celebrated holder of the post of Chief Fire Officer was Captain Massey Shaw, who held the job until 1891. The service grew rapidly under Shaw and his achievements were widely admired. In *Iolanthe* Gilbert and Sullivan praised his work:

> *"O Captain Shaw*
> *Could thy Brigade*
> *With cold cascade*
> *Quench my great love, I wonder."*

CHURCHES, CATHEDERALS AND CHAPELS

The churches were slow to make provision for the area's growing population. In 1750 there were three Anglican parishes – St Saviour, Christ Church and St George the Martyr – and a handful of Nonconformist chapels near the river. By the outbreak of World War I, there were two Cathedrals, nine Anglican parishes, two Roman Catholic parishes and at least nine Nonconformist churches. The changes that led to this situation were neither even in time nor across the different denominations.

The new Anglican parishes were: St Peter, Sumner Street (established 1846), a daughter parish of St Saviour; All Hallows, Copperfield St (1876), a daughter parish of St Saviour and Christ Church; and St Michael and All Angels, Lant Street (1881), St Alphege (1871), St Paul, Westminster Bridge Road (1858) and St Jude, St George's Road (1850), all daughter parishes of St George the Martyr.

St Alphege started as a mission church of St George. The mission had its first premises in a nearby building that had formerly housed a pub called the "Shamrock". The establishment of the

Above top: Southwark Cathedral, 1840.
Above: Surrey Chapel, Blackfriars Road, 1816.

St. George's R. C. Cathedral, Southwark.

St George's Roman Catholic Cathedral, c.1908.

parish owed much to the zeal and fearless drive of the founding vicar, Alfred Goulden, who also founded an order of Anglican nuns, the Sisters of the Reparation, and established their convent next to the church. The church building dates from 1882. The parish covered the poorest and roughest part of Bankside and the detailed description of the area in the parish annual report for 1883 clearly shows the amount of need. To the parish's great credit, in addition to usual parochial activities, such as a Sunday School, it made very practical provisions for the poor of the area. It established a Home for Working Boys, which provided accommodation for homeless working boys or orphans, and later a home for working girls, which was on Blackfriars Road. There was a working men's club, with games and reading material – this was attended by about 50 people per night – and a creche to ease the burden on mothers and improve standards of child care.

The area also went through changes in its Anglican diocesan structure. In 1877 Southwark became part of the diocese of Rochester, and the ancient link with Winchester and its bishops, who had had their palace on Bankside, was ended. The Diocese of Rochester was particularly active in its support for the mission or settlement movement, which provided much-needed social care in the poorer parts of south London. In 1905 a new Diocese of Southwark was created and, as detailed in Chapter 1, St Saviour's Church was given the additional status of a cathedral. Its full title became the Cathedral church of St Saviour and St Mary Overy.

While the Anglican Church was slow to respond to the need for extra places of worship, the Nonconformist churches were much quicker. This was partly due to the long tradition of Nonconformity in the area and partly because they were not hampered by a hierarchical diocesan structure. By 1750 there were a number of Nonconformist churches already in existence close to the river. Other places of worship included the Surrey Chapel, which stood on Blackfriars Road at the junction with Charlotte Street, now Union Street. This was built in 1782 and was the home of the preacher Rowland Hill. Like the Rotunda, it was octagonal in shape – supposedly to prevent the devil from hiding in the corners. Rowland Hill attracted large congregations and the building was used for preaching and worship until 1881. The Union Street (Methodist) Independent Chapel was erected in 1787 as a new home for the congregation that had previously met in Deadman's Place.

Stamford Street Unitarian Chapel was built in 1821 to provide a home for two existing congregations, one from Westminster and the other from Southwark. It stood on the south side of Stamford Street just inside the boundary with Lambeth at the corner of Broadwall. It was an imposing, heavy, classical building. Its congregation expanded through the 19th century and the building was enlarged in 1861, 1882 and 1897. It was used for worship until World War II. Its portico, which is supported by six Doric pillars, still stands and provides a curious screen for the London Nautical School playground behind.

A number of chapels were built on Borough Road, including the Baptist Surrey Tabernacle of 1838 and a General Baptist Chapel of 1839. One unexpected place of worship is the Welsh Congregational Chapel, just off Southwark Bridge Road. This was built in 1872-73 to provide services in the Welsh language for the large Welsh community who lived in the area. The congregation had been established in 1806 and had previously met in a chapel in Little Guildford Street.

The longest established cathedral in Bankside and St George's Fields is not the Anglican Cathedral at London Bridge but the Roman Catholic Cathedral of St George, on St George's Road. It was established as a cathedral in 1850. There had been a Roman Catholic place of worship in Bankside since at least 1786, when a room in Bandy Leg Walk (now Great Guildford Street) was used for Mass. This was one of only a very few public and independent Roman Catholic chapels in London – most Catholic places of worship were attached to the London embassies of foreign countries, so protecting themselves from anti-Roman Catholic feeling prevalent at the time.

In 1793 the congregation moved to a newly built chapel dedicated to St George (after the name of the Anglican parish in which it stood) in London Road, and by 1814 it claimed to have a congregation of more than 5,000. The chapel's work was boosted by the passing of the Catholic Emancipation Act in 1829, which lifted all remaining restrictions on Roman Catholic worship, and the appointment in the same year of Father Thomas Doyle as the senior priest. In 1830 Father Doyle estimated his congregation at 15,000. In 1839 a new site on St George's Road was purchased and work started on a much larger new church. Augustus Welby Pugin, the most famous name in the Victorian Gothic school of church architecture, designed the building, but his original design was not completed because money ran out before the spire could be built. His design was criticised by some for its lavish scale and ornament. The church was opened in 1848 and became a cathedral two years later. It was the first Roman Catholic cathedral in London and was in the first series of cathedrals established in England and Wales after the re-establishment of a diocesan structure in 1850. The parish of the Most Precious Blood in O'Meara Street was established in 1892, having started its existence as a mission church of St George's Cathedral.

Despite this flurry of church and chapel building it would be wrong to assume that the area's population was particularly keen to worship. The 1851 religious census suggests only 16 per cent of the population attended Anglican churches and the vicar of St Alphege estimated a congregation of 400 from a parish of 8,000 – he also described his flock as heathen. A higher proportion of Roman Catholics attended Mass – in the 1886 religious census of London 4,900 attended Mass at the cathedral (certainly half of the Catholic population) while the total attendance at the other 13 Anglican and Nonconformist churches was only slightly more at 5,700.

Nor were churches always seen as welcome. Henry Bateson, Medical Officer of Health for St George's, asked of churches in 1860: "considered as a specific remedy for the evils which now afflict us … I would seriously ask what avails such a remedy? The poor cannot go into them; will not go into them; and if they did, what benefit would be likely to follow?"

DAILY LIFE

MORTALITY AND CRIME

While high levels of church attendance do not guarantee high morals, the low levels of worship in the area are reflected in its lawless and seemingly immoral nature. The 1883 St Alfege's Mission report said that 50 per cent of poorer residents had convictions, adding that "the police come down here in companies. No solitary constable would venture where we have been to-night." Violence was common:

> "The bosom friends of yesterday will be fighting with brickbats, or even knives, within a few hours, and to-morrow will be sharing a pot of ale … A whole street would turn out in the morning armed with stones and bludgeons, to fight a pitched battle with another street that had offended them. On such occasions the police would prudently keep out of the way."

In 1880 St Saviour's Medical Officer of Health reported 28 deaths caused by violence; each year there were high numbers of accidental infant deaths in suspicious circumstances. It is reasonable to speculate that a fair number of the victims were unwanted.

Equally Charles Booth in his revision to the poverty survey visited each street in the district (usually in the company of a policeman) and commented "Drunk and disorderly cases, juvenile thieves, van draggers and racecourse roughs and a few prostitutes come from the Fair Street area." Many sources comment on the debilitating and degrading effects of drink.

Nor did sexual morals seem to be anything near our image of the Victorian period. St Alphege's parish commented that there were many teenage marriages and much living and having children out of wedlock: "There is no honour attached to marriage, and no shame to concubinage." Well into the 20th century many of the common lodging houses were no more than brothels.

RECREATION AND ENTERTAINMENT

In the 18th and 19th centuries the tradition of Bankside as a place of recreation and entertainment for Londoners continued. In 18th-century England there was a vogue for spas and the supposed medicinal properties of mineral water. In 1730 the "Dog and Duck" tavern in St George's Fields claimed to have found a source of mineral water and started to advertise itself as a spa. It became known as "St George's Spa" and the waters were highly valued; they were both consumed and bathed in. It must be doubtful if the waters came from a genuine spring, for there is no change in the geology of the area that could produce one. It is more likely the Hedgers, who ran the tavern, had diverted the contents of one of the numerous ditches on the fields. Writing in the 1850s, William Rendle was particularly scathing about the authenticity of the water source. The properties of the water alone were insufficient to realise the Hedgers' ambitions for the site, and the "Dog and Duck" diversified, providing other forms of entertainment. There was music, a tea garden, food and drink and later skittles and bowls. There were also suggestions that the spa was a cover for diversions of a less than moral sort. By the late 18th century, the site had become notoriously rowdy and there were calls for it to be closed down. But it continued to be used as a spa until 1799 when it closed. The building was demolished in 1811 to make way for the Bethlem Hospital.

There was another medicinal spa-cum-recreation ground called Finch's Grotto on a site just west of the modern Southwark Bridge Road, near its junction with Sawyer Street. This was established by Thomas Finch in the 1760s and, along with its waters, provided the inevitable series of evening entertainment, refreshments and music. A later proprietor, Mr Williams, who then gave his name to the business, added dances and fireworks to the list of entertainments. In 1773 the grotto and gardens were demolished and in 1777 the site was sold and was used for the site of a new workhouse for St Saviour's parish.

Other places of open-air entertainment were the Flora or Mount Gardens on Westminster Bridge Road, which was operating in the very late 18th century, and the Restoration or Spring Garden at the northern end of St George's Fields, which was in operation in the late 17th century.

The area of Blackfriars Road and St George's Circus became an important centre of indoor entertainment. The first places were not theatres, as might be supposed, but circuses, which put on sensational equestrian shows. The first of these and the first in the country was Astleys in Westminster Bridge Road, which was established in 1770. In 1782 one of the horsemen from Astleys, Charles Hughes, along with Charles Dibden, a songwriter, established the Royal Circus and Equestrian Philharmonic Academy just north of St George's Circus. This was burned down in 1803 and, after rebuilding, was converted into the Surrey Theatre, one of the most successful of London's popular theatres. It put on a wide variety of plays – from Shakespeare, through adaptations of Dickens to melodramas and pantomime. The Surrey continued to put on productions until 1920 when it became a cinema. It was pulled down in 1934 and the site was used for an extension to the Royal Opthalmic Hospital.

London's earliest Victorian music halls were in Lambeth and North Southwark. They evolved from informal entertainments in pubs; communal sing-songs or performances by singers and comic sketches. Some landlords went further than just using a separate room and built large concert halls. The most important of these in the Bankside area was the South London Palace in London Road, which dates from 1860. It could seat 4,000. There were other music halls on the site of the "Winchester" pub on Southwark Bridge Road and the "Raglan", or "Borough" on Union Street. The heyday of the music hall was the last 20 years of the 19th century. There were many in authority who viewed large numbers of the working classes enjoying themselves, and the entertainments that they enjoyed, with the same suspicion and distaste that their 17th-century counterparts had felt for the Bankside theatres of that era. Halls – particularly smaller ones, which could afford to run greater risks – were inspected for indecent songs and sketches, drunkenness and lewd behaviour. A condition of the licence of the "Surrey Vaudeville" on Blackfriars Road was that it could not sell alcohol. Many of the smaller halls became cinemas in the early years of the 20th century.

For many the only public meeting place, recreation and escape from the rigours of work, poor housing and family was the public house. Working-class areas of Victorian London were exceedingly well provided with beer houses and pubs. In 1904 there were 157 in the area, about one for each 450 people. In addition to music, pubs provided other entertainment such as gambling and sport (particularly boxing), and provided a cover for the activities of prostitutes. Excessive drinking was seen as a major social problem – Victorian levels of beer and spirit consumption were much greater than ours.

The area formed part of the route for two impressive royal parades: Queen Victoria's Diamond Jubilee in 1897 and the coronation of Edward VII in 1902. These provided opportunities to demonstrate widespread, enthusiastic and genuine patriotism.

Borough Road during the procession at Queen Victoria's Diamond Jubilee, 1897.

CHAPTER 4

Industrial rise and fall, and the birth of modern Bankside: 1914-2001

Modern Bankside and St George's Fields is largely a 20th-century landscape, a product of five main themes of the area's recent history. These are: the continued improvement in public health and housing conditions following World War I; the ongoing industrialisation of the area and its revival after World War II; the destruction caused by World War II; the decline in industry and population in postwar years; and the regeneration of the post-industrial landscape in very recent years.

WORLD WAR I

People from the Bankside area enlisted in great numbers to fight in World War I. The recruiting sergeant's call to patriotism fell on receptive ears in working-class areas, and for many army life offered an escape from squalor and poverty. Many were recruited to the area's local regiment, the 24th London Regiment, based at Braganza Street, Walworth. As the slaughter of the war became apparent, the practice of enlisting men from the same area to a single regiment ceased and recruits were posted to regiments from all parts of the country.

The number of war memorials in the area are a poignant reminder of the human cost of the war. The municipal memorial stands outside the town hall on Walworth Road, but most major institutions and firms erected a plaque in memory of lost colleagues: examples include one in St George's Roman Catholic Cathedral, a window in Southwark Cathedral dedicated to workers from the Oxo company and another at Barclay Perkins Brewery. Several men from the area were honoured with conspicuous bravery awards. The best known is Lance Corporal Leonard Keyworth of the 24th London Regiment, who was awarded the Victoria Cross for his bravery in an attack in 1915.

Keyworth's association with the area was as a member of the local regiment; he was originally from Lincolnshire. Despite this, Bankside people took him to their heart and a street – between Borough Road and Southwark Bridge Road – was named after him.

World War I also had a major effect on the lives of those who remained at home, far from the front line. Industrial output increased and diversified to support the war effort – for example, the Borough Council made its machinery available to assist with shell manufacture. Women performed manual labour traditionally done by men, and gained new skills, their own income and independence. Londoners had an unwelcome introduction to a new aspect of warfare – air raids. The damage caused by air raids in World War I was tiny compared to that caused in World War II – the only notable World War I air raid in the Bankside area was in 1917, when three people were killed at the British & Bennington (Blue Cross) Tea Co at 118 Southwark Street. But the population saw that they were entirely unprotected and the raids did immense damage to public confidence and morale.

A legacy of World War I was the Imperial War Museum, which came to the area in 1936. The idea for a museum to collect, display and interpret material and documents related to war (originally World War I) was conceived in 1917. It first opened to the public at Crystal Palace in 1920 and then transferred to South Kensington until 1935, when it moved into premises in the St George's Fields area that had been vacated by the Bethlem Hospital and was opened by the Duke and Duchess of York. Its collection was put in safe keeping during World War II and the museum was reopened in 1947. A major fire damaged the dome and the library reading room in 1968. More recently, the museum has expanded. Its remit is "to collect, preserve and display material and information with a bearing on two World Wars and other military operations since 1914, in which Great Britain or other members of the Commonwealth have been involved". It interprets this brief widely and many of its most successful exhibits have been concerned with the civilian and social aspects of wartime.

IMPROVEMENTS FOLLOWING WORLD WAR I

HEALTH AND HOUSING

After World War I the municipal authorities – the Borough of
Southwark, the London County Council (LCC), the Corporation of
London and the Board of Guardians – sought with vigour to
tackle the problems of housing and public health. They were
prompted and assisted by public opinion, made more apparent
and vocal by the widening of the franchise in and after 1918; by
central government, which laid the legislative framework; and by
one important local factor, an overall drop in population. While
the numbers living in the area near the river had been falling
since 1861, the population of the area overall peaked in 1901 at
about 59,400 and fell for the next 90 years (in comparison the
same area in 1991 was home to about 6,500). The fall was
prompted by the loss of men and the families they would have
had in World War I, the continued expansion of industry and,
from the 1920s onwards, the rehousing policies of the LCC. By
1939 about 35,000 lived in Bankside and St George's Fields, a fall
of 45 per cent in just under 40 years.

The LCC's main contribution to housing was rehousing people
from central London on estates it built away from the centre.
This was a practical solution to the problem of overcrowding as
there was simply insufficient space in the inner areas and
improved public transport and shorter working hours now
allowed those with steady jobs to travel to their places of work.
Many were removed to new large estates built on garden suburb
lines on the outskirts of London, such as at Downham in
Lewisham or Becontree. The LCC also built other schemes closer
to London such as at Deptford and Dog Kennel Hill in
Camberwell; although these homes were in purpose-built blocks
rather than houses, they proved to be more popular as they were
closer to the places from which people had moved.

The Borough of Southwark provided relatively little social
housing in the area, preferring to let the LCC take the initiative.
Of the 22 metropolitan boroughs, only seven had provided fewer
rooms by 1936 than Southwark.

By contrast, and perhaps unexpectedly, the City of London set about providing council housing. Although the City had few residents within its own boundaries who needed rehousing, many people lived in very poor accommodation on land the City (or more strictly the Bridge House Committee) owned. In Bankside they built three estates: Sumner Buildings, Sumner Street (1931-32), which was built on land bought to be used as part of the approach to a planned but aborted new Thames bridge; Stopher House, Silex Street (1935); and Pakeman House, Pocock Street (1939). The Church Commissioners built seven blocks of flats at the corner of Union Street and Great Guildford Street in the late 1930s.

These changes further decreased the proportion of local people living in private rented accommodation to about 75 per cent of the total. Above average numbers of people were still living in overcrowded homes or in illegally occupied underground or basement rooms, and there were complaints about the quality of management of some of the tenement blocks. Despite this, in 1939, the quality of private rented accommodation was much improved on the position in 1900.

Harry Cole, later a policeman and author of numerous best-selling humorous reminiscences of his life and work in the area, recalled his childhood in the 1930s. His family moved to Queen's Buildings, Scovell Road, in the mid-1930s from Collinson Street:

> "The flat consisted of just two rooms with an outside toilet that led off a small balcony ... reached via a steep, narrow and damp staircase ... Mum and Dad slept in the front room with all the best furniture, and I slept in a corner of the kitchen with a ceiling-to-floor curtain draped around my bed ... it had one thing that my mum craved – it had electricity!"

Previously the family shared a small terraced house with two other families.

Great improvements were made in the area's public health. Mortality fell steadily from 16 deaths per 1,000 of the population per year in 1907, to 13 per 1,000 in 1936. Much greater advances were made in infant mortality ("infants" were those under the age of one), which fell from 142 per 1,000 in 1907, to 95 per 1,000 in 1919, and 59 per 1,000 in 1936. (These figures were still above the London average.) Much of the credit for this achievement must go to the Borough of Southwark, which was charged with providing preventative healthcare to its population. It did this through its health centre in Walworth Road and clinics, including ones in Surrey Square and Pocock Street. The health centre and clinics were particularly active in the fields of maternity and child welfare and in dealing with tuberculosis. Both notifications and deaths from this disease fell by almost half between 1920 and 1939. The Boards of Guardians, who ran public hospitals until 1930, and the LCC, who ran them thereafter, also played an important role. They were of course assisted by overall improvements in food hygiene, the provision of a clean and permanent water supply, an efficient sewage system and routine vaccinations against diseases that had previously needlessly killed many.

PARKS, OPEN SPACES AND RECREATION

Bankside has always been short of parks and open spaces. Harry Cole's playground was the streets:

> "stealing rides was probably the most popular sport among young boys at the time. In theory this activity was very dangerous, but in practice it was enormous fun. Two or three boys would wait at a junction or set of traffic lights until a suitable open-backed lorry stopped. Then, as the truck moved away and gathered speed, they would rush out into the road and leap up to grab the tailboard of the now fast-departing vehicle. Each boy would then have to use his own judgement of the best moment to drop off. The last one to let go was considered the winner ... The river was probably the greatest of the lures ... Great colliers of the Gas Light and Coke Co would determinedly plough their way through the waters on an apparent collision course with the centre spans of Southwark Bridge. Then, yards from seeming disaster, the smoking black funnel would hinge back and lie flat along the deck of the boat. For any kid leaning precariously over the parapet of the bridge, this would mean a lungful of smoke and a faceful of soot. A small price to pay for so rewarding a sight."

A major addition to the area's meagre open spaces was made in 1936 with the opening of Geraldine Mary Harmsworth Park, previously the grounds of the Bethlem Hospital. The grounds had been purchased by Viscount Rothermere, proprietor of the *Daily Mail,* and converted to a public park at his expense; he had given the site to the LCC, which ran it thereafter. It is named after his mother, who raised Rothermere and his family in circumstances of poverty and discomfort. The park, of 14 acres, increased the amount of open space in the area fourfold. However, it did little for Harry Cole who said "Bedlam Park was excruciatingly boring: a flat, square open space with nothing to fire the imagination of an honest street urchin." For Cole and many other children, matters improved with the building of a large paddling pool in the park in 1938.

The Ring

One of London's more unusual sporting venues was the boxing arena "The Ring" on Blackfriars Road. It was remarkable because the building had previously been used as a chapel – Rowland Hill's Surrey Chapel – and because it was managed by a woman, Bella Burge. The Ring was used for boxing from 1910 to 1940. It was the proprietor's aim that ordinary working men should be able to afford admission; uncommon among London's venues, but realistic given the area's population. Its prestige must have been raised by the attendance of the Duke of Windsor in 1928 – although he had visited incognito on previous occasions. Bella Burge managed the Ring after her husband's death in 1918 until the building's demolition by bombing in 1940. Many of boxing's biggest names, national and international, danced on its canvas.

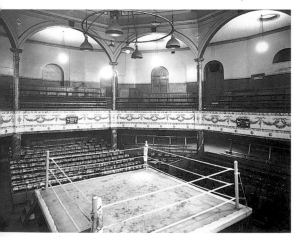

The interior of The Ring, Blackfriars Road.

TRANSPORT

The prewar years also saw improvements in transport. Southwark Bridge was rebuilt in 1921, greatly increasing its capacity. Public transport improved with the introduction of motor buses. And the motor van replaced the horse and cart as the preferred mode of commercial transport. Blackfriars Road was a particularly busy tram route.

The Bakerloo Line's depot was built at the corner of St George's Road and London Road; it still stands there today, hidden behind high walls but a landmark when viewed from the air. In 1909 plans were made for a major new bridge and associated roads to link the Elephant & Castle with the Angel, Islington. The new crossing was to be called St Paul's Bridge and was to follow a course just downstream of where the Millennium Bridge now stands. The City acquired land for the approaches, but insufficient funds were raised for the scheme and it was abandoned in 1929.

INDUSTRIAL EXPANSION AFTER WORLD WAR I

Southwark as a manufacturing and industrial centre expanded in the years up to World War II. During this period, about one third of the land was given over to some sort of commercial concern. At the same time, the character of Bankside's industries was changing. Some of the larger firms were leaving the area, for example marine engineers John Rennie who as early as 1890 moved from Holland Street to Deptford to take advantage of larger sites where the noise and pollution they generated were less of an issue.

FOOD

Food and drink firms expanded vigorously. Barclay Perkins, who ran the Anchor Brewery, took over other breweries, such as the Royal Brewery at Brentford, Style and Winch and the Dartford Brewery Company. Correspondingly, the hop trade flourished in the early 20th century but in 1932 the Hop Marketing Board (HMB) was formed to assume the duties of the hop factors.

Boning meat at J Sainsbury's new factory, 1936.

There was no longer bargaining between factor and merchant and the crop was valued instead by the HMB. The trade suffered a further blow in World War II when 25 of the 37 London warehouses were destroyed by bombing.

The most important food producer and retailer associated with Bankside is J.Sainsbury; the company's Stamford Street address is printed on the packaging of food sold across the country. The firm expanded rapidly in the first half of the 20th century and all the central elements of their operations – management, clerical, buying, staff training, warehousing and major sections of food production and distribution – were run from Bankside. In 1913 Sainsbury's opened its new headquarters building, Stamford House, on the corner of Bennett Street (now Rennie Street). This contained senior management (mostly members of the Sainsbury family) and clerical and purchasing staff on the top floor, warehouses and packing areas on the middle floors and distribution on the ground floor. In 1932, 945 staff were employed at the premises. On the opposite side of the street were the kitchens, although these were replaced by a new factory, opened in 1936, principally for the manufacture of sausages and pies. Designed by Sir Owen Williams (architect also of Wembley Stadium, the *Daily Express* building in Fleet Street and the Boot's factory in Nottingham) it was far ahead of its time. One of the first buildings in London to be constructed on the "flat slab principle" (the weight of the floors are supported by twin rows of internal columns), it was altered to act as office and laboratory accommodation in 1975 and was re-named Rennie House. Bacon was cured in other premises in Union Street.

Prominent on Southwark's riverfront today is the OXO Tower. The famous beef cube was an adaptation of Baron Justus von Liebig's beef extract, LEMCO, formulated in 1840 and a firm favourite of Florence Nightingale, Scott of the Antarctic, and Alcock and Brown; it was even taken by Stanley on his search for Dr Livingstone in Africa. OXO Ltd was formed in 1914 to market the product in the UK. The company developed a solid cube of the beef extract that sold for one penny, and so was born the famous OXO cube – an immediate success. The price remained at one penny until 1952. No one knows how the name came about but there is a story that a dock worker chalked the letters O-X-O on a crate as a private code to distinguish it from other products.

The parent company's London wharf was originally in Limehouse, but the lease there was due to run out in 1930 and a new warehouse was needed. Accordingly, the site of the Post Office's power station, just west of Blackfriars Bridge, was acquired and a new wharf of nine floors and floor space of 250,000 square feet (23,000 square metres) was built in 1928. The OXO Tower is 202 feet (60 metres) in height and at the time of its construction was the second tallest building in London. Advertising was not permitted at such a height but the company got round this by a splendidly crafty manoeuvre. The top windows are shaped to form the letters OXO, illuminated by a light shining from inside. Afterwards there were instructions to demolish the tower, but what was done was done!

There were other food producers in the area. At 57 Great Suffolk Street was the pungent Southwark Bacon Drying Co. Opened as The Empire Bacon Curing Co in 1914, it was close to the riverside wharves such as Hibernia (Montague Close), Crown (off Bankside) and Union and Nelson's (Upper Ground), where imported meat was landed. The sides of bacon, received from the wharves, were first hosed with warm water, then dusted with pea flour to improve their final appearance. They were then hooked onto bars within the oven ready for smoking – as many as 300 sides could be loaded into each oven. Hardwood sawdust was brought in from nearby Brixton, spread on the floor and ignited. As the temperature increased, fat dripped onto the floor from the hanging sides, adding to the smoke. A full stove would have three successive firings over 36 hours.

ELECTRICITY, ENGINEERING AND PRINTING

Electricity generation in the area expanded as a result of increased demand for electricity from industry coupled with rising numbers of domestic customers. The invention of the steam turbine by C.A.Parsons in the late 19th century had an enormous impact on the electricity supply industry. The original Bankside power station of 1891 was expanded. It housed a Parsons 2,500KW turbo-alternator replacing some of the earlier engine-driven machines. More turbines quickly followed and by 1915 capacity had risen to 34,500KW. After the war expansion continued with more boilers and turbines added and a concentration on alternating current supply. Before the coming of the National Grid, Bankside was responsible for its own distribution but later teamed up with the neighbouring County of London Electric Supply Co and the Charing Cross,

Bankside Power Station under construction. A view of 1952 from Skin Market Place, off New Globe Walk. A pen and ink drawing by Geoffrey Fletcher.

West End and City Co to interchange current and provide better security of supply for Londoners. Then in 1934 the station came under the direction of the Central Electricity Board with a grid substation built at Bankside with connection to the National Grid. The eventual plant capacity for prewar Bankside was 85,000KW with two 15MW, five 10MW and one 5MW sets operating at a steam pressure of 270psi.

The station continued to serve Londoners during the war. The night of 29 December 1940 was the worst night of the Blitz when convoys of German bombers hit London in wave after wave. It was also a memorable night for the power station – fuel oil tanks and other plant were lost, but remarkably the main body of the station was unharmed.

The original Bankside power station is now long gone but a extraordinary incident occurred during its heyday in the interwar years. A 12-year-old boy was playing by the river water suction pumps when he lost his footing and fell in. A workman saw the accident and immediately raised the alarm and the pump was switched off. The boy, meanwhile, had been thundered, totally submerged, for well over a minute through the 3-foot (90-cm) diameter entry pipe, through a couple of hairpin bends and along a distance of 50 yards (45 metres) to a screened chamber under vacuum. The vacuum was turned off but it was 20 minutes before workmen were able to lift the cover of the chamber and perform what they thought would be the gruesome task of removing the body of a dead child. To their astonishment, when the cover was removed a loud cry was heard and there before the workmen's eyes was the adventurous lad, clinging to the screen with his head just out of the water. After the briefest of hospital visits he was pronounced "none the worse for his experience" and sent home wrapped in a blanket.

Although many of the engineering firms had left the area, heavy industry was still represented by the City Lead Works of Grey and Marten, just east of Southwark Bridge, where the *Financial Times* building now stands. The works' chimneys were a prominent landmark, but were demolished in 1980. The firm imported lead, mainly from Australia. Before World War II it was unloaded from lighters to the riverside wharf. In the 1920s, lead sheet was produced by melting the imported pig metal in pots beneath the arches of the bridge and then allowing it to run out onto a bed of 7 ton capacity to give lead sheet up to 9 inches (22 centimetres) thick. Lead pipes were made by pouring the molten metal into a cylinder. After cooling, a ram was forced down the cylinder by a vertical hydraulic press to extrude the lead in pipe form which was then wound onto a drum. Lead is a highly toxic metal and after World War II demand fell for its use in pipes and sheet and the firm then diversified into the manufacture of lead solder.

Printing remained very active. During the General Strike of 1926, the directors of Burrups were forced to operate the plant themselves and even printed the *Daily Express*, which they claimed at the time was the only national newspaper to announce that the Duchess of York had given birth to a daughter, now Queen Elizabeth II. As well as performing financial printing, the firm produced *Boys' Own Paper* and saucy seaside postcards. On the night of 29 December 1940, in common with many other buildings, 114 Southwark Street was reduced to a shell. The London School of Printing moved to Stamford Street in 1922 and to its present site at the Elephant & Castle in the mid-1960s.

The main route for the supply of raw materials for the Bankside firms was the River Thames. Virtually the whole riverfront was given over to cranes with warehouses behind. Goods were unloaded from the ships that had brought the imports from overseas onto smaller lighters, which carried them to the wharves. The lightermen modestly called these vessels "punts" and their great skill and strength enable them to power and control a 50-ton lighter with a single oar. There were generations of lightermen working on the river. One example was the Harris family of Park Street. Harry Harris in his autobiography *Under Oars* described his childhood and work. Of his childhood play time he said:

> "Our chief attraction was Bankside. This was out of bounds to me and almost all children, owing to the unrestricted opportunities for getting 'overboard'. I soon learnt every inch of the Bank and knew where to hide if Father was seen or reported....With friends, chiefly sons of Watermen and Lightermen, we soon made free of boats that were not actually in use, so naturally we became boat minded at an early age."

Even the family's annual holiday was on board a boat. Of those that worked on the river he said:

> "As a class they were loyal to each other, jealous of the 'privilege' [freedom of the River], clannish as the clans, mildly tolerant of landsmen, benevolent to anyone in trouble. I could tell a lightermen anywhere Sunday or day clothes apparel"

The Great Depression
Bankside suffered more than other parts of London during the depression years of the 1930s. The area's less skilled workers were hit by a decline in the availability of casual work, especially in the docks and on the wharves as the dock registration scheme

and increased mechanisation on the wharves reduced the need for labour. In early 1934, when circumstances were at their worst, levels of unemployment approached 20 per cent in Bankside, compared to a London average of 15 per cent.

The poor received relief in two ways: unemployment benefit or handouts from the Boards of Guardians. The generosity of the Boards of Guardians in the years up to 1930, when they were abolished, contrasts strongly with the meaner policies of the LCC, which took on this responsibility at that time. The Borough of Southwark also did its bit to alleviate unemployment by using its public libraries as employment exchanges in the early years of the century.

WORLD WAR II

Like the rest of inner-London, Bankside suffered badly during World War II. The war caused destruction and disruption on a scale never seen before. The area offered a high concentration of both industrial and civilian targets and few opportunities for effective protection against air raids. In the Borough of Southwark as a whole nearly 1,000 people were killed.

The Borough Council was responsible for coordinating civil defence. It was handicapped in this respect as the low-lying and marshy land offered little opportunity for deeply dug shelters, the only form of protection from direct hits. Instead, the few people who had gardens made Anderson shelters (makeshift tunnel constructions of timber and galvanised steel partly covered in earth). For the rest the Council provided a number of hastily-built surface or shallow-dug shelters made from brick. Even then it had a problem as the area had almost no open space on which these could be built. The one exception was on its parks and there was a shelter for 1,000 people at Geraldine Mary Harmsworth Park and one for 400 at Nelson Square. There were shelters at individual tenement blocks such as the one for 800 people at Peabody Buildings, Blackfriars Road. The shelters provided by the Corporation of London for its tenants in Sumner Buildings were noted for their good facilities, having beds and toilets. Individual firms were also required to

provide protection for their
employees but they did
so less promptly than the
Borough's public shelters.
The firm Beck and Politzer
in Southwark Street had
a shelter for 600.

The one shelter that offered
real protection was in a
disused railway tunnel that
ran under Borough High
Street and north to the City.
It was called The Deep (it
was 70" underground) and
though in times of danger

Bomb damage in Southwark Street, 1941.
The location is the junction with Thrale Street;
Southwark Cathedral is in the background.

conditions were often overcrowded and squalid (it had a reportedly
high number of drunks and few toilets) it offered secure protection
to up to 14,000 people after it opened in June 1940.

The other precaution taken against threatened air-raids was
civilian evacuation. This was organised by the London County
Council through its schools and at the onset of war in September
1939 about half the area's children were evacuated. Through a
combination of unhappy experiences while away, and an almost
total lack of enemy action in the early months of the war, most
had returned home by January 1940.

The air raids of the blitz, which started on September 7 1940,
caused massive destruction. Direct hits on shelters caused the
highest number of deaths, such as in Ewer Street on 10 September,
which killed 20 people, including two wardens, and in Keyworth
Street in on 27 December, which killed ten. The single worst
incident of the blitz was a hit on Queen's Buildings, on 16 October,
which killed 38. The intensity of air raids diminished between
1941 and 1944 but then recommenced with the arrival of VI, a
pilotless flying bomb, nicknamed the doodlebug, and later the
VII, a much fiercer rocket-powered bomb. A VI, which landed in
Union Street on 19 June 1944, was the single most deadly
incident in the area killing over 50 people.

THE POST WAR YEARS

The end of the war heralded a new era of government intervention in planning. A London-wide plan, the Abercrombie Plan, had detailed proposals for Southwark and areas like it, close to central London. Locally the proposals concerned the rebuilding of industry, an obvious and urgent priority; the development of the south bank as a cultural and office centre, particularly for government departments; an expansion in open spaces; and policies that would drastically reduce the population of the area. The first of these was successful in the short term, but was a false dawn, as by the 1980s most industry had left. The cultural element of the second was achieved through the building of the Festival Hall and other venues on the Festival of Britain site on the South Bank. Offices were built in Southwark, but the process nearly became a monster out of control. Finally population did fall, but to much lower levels than anticipated.

INDUSTRIAL REVIVAL AND DECLINE

The first priority for industry after the war was to rebuild as quickly as possible. Apart from the debate about the future development of another power station on Bankside (and this was more to do with the threat to the newly opened-up views of St Paul's Cathedral from the south) there was little questioning as to whether industry had a future in the area. Many areas needed rebuilding and the necessary work was undertaken with vigour. New warehouses such as those behind the OXO Tower and printing works for Her Majesty's Stationery Office (HMSO) in Pocock Street were built.

Probably the most important building on Bankside today is Tate Modern, which was built after the war as a new power station for London. The authorities had realised that a new power station was needed as early as 1939, but then the war intervened and plans for a new station at Bankside were put on hold. After the war the shortage of power reached crisis proportions and permission was sought to alleviate this in 1946 by building a conventional coal-fired station. There were immediate objections and a public enquiry was held. Opposition concentrated on two issues. The first was that the power station would hamper the view of St Paul's Cathedral, its vista now newly opened up by wartime bombing. It was also anticipated that the sulphurous fumes emitted by the stack would drift across the river and damage the Cathedral's stonework. The second difficulty was that the station would not fit in with the Abercrombie Plan, one of whose aims was to remedy what it called the "maldistribution and deficiencies" of open space in London by providing more public recreational areas. The plan's scheme for the South Bank envisaged a park for Bankside with commercial building behind. Prominent in opposition to the construction of the new power station were the LCC, the City Corporation, Southwark Borough Council and the Dean and Chapter of St Paul's Cathedral.

However, their efforts were to no avail and permission for the construction of the power station was granted by Lewis Silkin, Minister for Town and Country Planning, with the proviso that oil be used to fire the station instead of coal and that the flue gases be washed to prevent the emission of sulphurous fumes. The issues were debated in both the House of Commons and the House of Lords. In the Lords the scheme was likened to "introducing an alligator into a water lily pond" but the Lord Chancellor, Viscount Jowitt, early to appreciate the beauty of power stations, retorted "this may be the largest and most beautiful lily in the pond." The architect chosen for Bankside power station, on the recommendation of the engineering firm of Mott Hay and Anderson, was Sir Giles Gilbert Scott. From a family of eminent architects, Scott is best known for his design of Liverpool's Anglican Cathedral, the elegant and graceful Waterloo Bridge, parts of Battersea Power Station and the red telephone kiosk. His other prominent building in Southwark is the Salvation Army training centre on Denmark Hill.

Work on the power station commenced in 1948. The electricity supply industry was nationalised in the same year and Bankside, in common with all power stations in England and Wales, came under the direction of the British Electricity Authority. In the initial stages two turbines of 60MW were installed. Later, in 1959, the original power station of the City of London Electric Lighting Company was closed and demolished. Work started the next day to make way for the second half of the Bankside station with the installation of a further 60MW generator and a much larger 120MW unit.

There were three special features that set Bankside power station apart. The first is its appearance, as a true "temple of power", which was the culmination of Sir Giles Scott's power station designs; most would agree that he fully met his brief, which was to design a building that harmonised with those existing and planned for the South Bank redevelopment. The second and third features lay in its technical design – to avoid dust and particulate smoke pollution, Bankside was the first large generating station to be fired solely by oil and a flue gas washing plant was incorporated to remove sulphur dioxide and other acid gases. Like Battersea Power Station, Bankside has four flues, but they are all combined into one central chimney.

Bankside Power Station received many distinguished visitors in its heyday – the 1960s and early 1970s. The Queen visited in 1962, Prince Charles in 1968 and the Lord Mayor of London in 1975. At this time the Central Electricity Generating Board ran all power stations in England and Wales and supplied power to the grid according to a system known as the "merit order" – the most efficient stations supplied power first, followed by older and hence less efficient stations that were used only when demand required. Bankside was always high up the list, particularly the later 120MW set which always featured in the top 20 most efficient generators. In autumn 1970 record output levels were broken twice. On 30 September 5,876,246 units were sent out over a 24-hour period, but then on 8 October the record was raised to 6,004,364 units.

In 1973 came the Arab-Israeli war, resulting in the oil price crisis of the mid-1970s. The oil-fired Bankside station never really recovered. It simply could not compete, in price terms, with larger coal-fired stations or with nuclear power. The final outcome was inevitable and after a period of gradual decline power generation at Bankside ceased in 1981.

There was no debate after the war about the need for a prompt return to activity on the riverside wharves. Writing in 1950,

Grace Golden, a long-standing resident and author of *Old Bankside,* described the events thus:

> "*After the paralysing effects of the last war, Bankside today is coming to life. The gloomy fronts of buildings, which for years have looked like unburied corpses, are receiving fresh coats of paint on doors and window frames. Cranes, which I thought permanently flattened against a wall, are swinging backwards and forwards, so pleased at their release that they scarcely wait to be relieved of their cargo before returning to replenish ... where I had expected to see a plain brick wall stood a cluster of enormous hoppers like giant toadstools on fragile stalks, receiving charges of gravel from a grab moving between them and the boat on the wharf.*"

The Port of London became very busy in the late 1950s when it exceeded its prewar activity by value, volume and proportion of national imports. It was not to last, however, and the rapid rundown and closure of the port was a major factor in the decline of manufacturing in the area. The closure was due to the use of much larger ships, containerisation and alternative means of transport and storage. Many of the Bankside warehouses closed. St Mary Overy's, Rosings' and Stave Wharves were three of Bankside's finest. A brave attempt was made to save St Mary Overy's Wharf, which at the time was a listed building. It stood to the west of St Mary Overie Dock (by convention, the dock is spelled differently to the wharf). There were plans to berth Captain Scott's *HMS Discovery,* the ship in which he sailed to the Antarctic, but in spite of the intervention of the local MP, Simon Hughes, who spoke up in Parliament for St Mary Overy's conservation, it was demolished in the 1980s.

St Mary Overy's Wharf and many other warehouses may have gone but there are still warehouses to be seen in Clink Street, Bear Gardens and Upper Ground, in Southwark Bridge Road at the Southwark Playhouse, and in Trundle Street and Vine Yard.

The hop trade, too, contracted. After the war, because of planning restraints, it proved difficult for merchants to rebuild their warehouses and instead the Hop Marketing Board built a vast

A busy wharf scene. A drawing by Grace Golden of 1929.

warehouse at Paddock Wood in Kent. The hop trade in Southwark
never really recovered and came to an abrupt end in 1972. Today
there remains much evidence of this once-flourishing trade. Apart

from the Hop Exchange itself, there also survives a decorative panel of hop gatherers at the former premises of W.H.LeMay at 67 Borough High Street (now Securicor). At 14 Union Street, Price Waterhouse Coopers have offices in a converted hop warehouse dating from 1853. Hop warehouses at 51-53 Southwark Street survive, as does part of Calvert's Buildings at 15 Southwark Street.

In 1955 Barclay Perkins merged with Courage and soon became a bottling plant, finally closing in 1982. The site was purchased by the Greater London Council (GLC, successor to the London County Council) for £2.5 million, so bringing to an end nearly 300 years of large-scale brewing in Bankside.

Bankside's pre-eminence in food processing also drew to a close. With the rundown of the wharves in the 1950s Sainsbury's was deprived of the source of many of its raw materials; it also found the Blackfriars site too cramped as a centre for distribution. By this time the chain had expanded significantly and had stores all over southern England that needed the prompt supply of an increasing range of fresh foods. By 1973 Sainsbury's warehousing, distribution and food processing had all moved from the area. The Southwark Bacon Drying Company fell victim to changing eating habits with a preference for unsmoked (green) bacon, forcing the company to close in 1980; the building still stands today at the corner of Pocock Street and a weather-beaten sign still proclaims "Bacon Smoking in Progress". Ashby Teas in Union Street ceased work in 1985 and Stevenson and Howell, the food essence makers in Bear Lane ceased work in 1973. Stevenson and Howell's records are in the collection at Southwark Local Studies Library.

Printing proved more resilient. After a number of years away from Southwark, Burrups returned to new premises in Lavington Street in 1959. In 1964 they were taken over by the Exchange Telegraph Company. The Pocock Street premises of St Stephen's Parliamentary Press, part of HMSO, opened in 1961 in the presence of the Lord Chancellor and the Speaker of the House of Commons. The new press printed not only the parliamentary record *Hansard* but also the *London Gazette,* as well as order papers, Bills and Acts and other printed matter for Parliament.

In the 1980s HMSO moved from Pocock Street to the Bricklayers' Arms. But Bankside's printing tradition is continued today with many small concerns still operating in the area.

COMMERCIAL OFFICES

Official policies that encouraged the building of office premises meant that new jobs were on offer in Bankside in the years after World War II. But the jobs were not in areas of work in which local people had skills or experience. A number of new offices were built to house government departments. Examples include St Christopher House (Southwark Street), built in 1959, and Orbit House (Blackfriars Road), designed by Richard Seifert, a name associated with many London office blocks. Orbit House was later home to the British Library's India Office Collection before its move to Euston Road in 1998. Dorset House, the pre-war headquarters of printing and publishing firm Illife & Son, on Stamford Street, is today used by H.M.Customs and Excise.

Businesses were also keen to take advantage of low land costs to build new offices. Unilever built themselves a new office block, United Africa House, on the south side of Blackfriars Bridge, partnering their main headquarters on the north. This, renamed Drury House, along with other buildings, was taken over by J.Sainsbury, which, in the late 1990s, was employing 4,000 people in the area. Lloyds Bank built its huge computing centre on Hopton Street in the early 1980s and at the same time the Post Office built a large addition to its telephone exchange of 1934 between Blackfriars Road and Hatfields. St Christopher House, the Lloyds Bank centre and the new telephone exchange are among the ugliest buildings in the whole of Southwark.

National and regional campaigning and voluntary organisations also took advantage of relatively low cost office space. Examples are the Electoral Reform Society, which has its headquarters in Chancel Street, the League Against Cruel Sports in Southwark Bridge Road and War on Want and drugs charity Hope (UK), both in Great Guildford Street, and the London Cycling Campaign, originally in Stamford Street and now also in Great Guildford Street.

The legal system, which has had such a long association with the area, returned in the early 1990s with the building of the new Blackfriars Crown Court on Pocock Street.

Artists were also attracted by low rents and large spaces in Bankside and a thriving artistic community developed in the 1970s and 1980s. Prominent members were sculptor Elizabeth Frink and film maker Derek Jarman, who shot much of his 1978 punk film *Jubilee* in the Bankside area.

Bankside's traditional association with printing has diversified into publishing and the area is now home to the wider media. Two national newspapers have their editorial headquarters on Bankside (although ironically they are printed elsewhere). These are Express Newspapers, which is based on the riverfront just east of Blackfriars Bridge, and the *Financial Times* – also on the riverfront just east of Southwark Bridge. Both moved to the area in the late 1980s, when the newspaper industry abandoned Fleet Street. IPC Magazines, which publishes many popular and trade periodicals, has its headquarters in King's Reach Tower, at the corner of Stamford Street and Hatfields. It has been in the area since 1976. It generates much ancillary work for local businesses and the area still has numerous photography labs, printers and print finishers.

The use of computers in publishing has ended the trade of the typesetter (who set metal characters to produce the image from which to print), but there are numerous small firms working in the new media and in e-commerce. A good example of this process is the conversion of the building at 156 Blackfriars Road. This had been the home of Wicks Rotary Type Casting and previously (from 1819) the Blackfriars Type Foundry. It was converted to become a centre for small businesses, using money provided by the City of London as part of the celebration of its 800th anniversary in 1986. Appropriately, its annexe in Glasshill Street was previously an ink factory.

Local residents have generally been hostile to large-scale office developments and a long battle was fought over the planned development of the riverfront Coin Street site, which is part in

Southwark and part in Lambeth. The owners of the site, Greycoat, had plans for a £200 million development of mainly offices to be housed in a series of curving slabs in the area between Stamford Street and Upper Ground. One aspect of their proposal was prophetic in that they included a giant ferris wheel. The plans met ferocious resistance from the Association of Waterloo Groups, a well-organised umbrella body of local residents, who argued that the site should include substantial amounts of social housing. Two public enquiries were held about Greycoat's proposals and at one time two conflicting sets of proposals had planning permission. The stalemate was broken by the GLC (who were also vigorously opposed to Greycoat); the GLC bought the freehold of the site from Greycoat for £2.7 million (a figure thought to be about twice its market value) and promptly sold it to Coin Street Community Builders (CSCB – the body that had evolved from the opposition groups) for £750,000.

CSCB developed the site to their plans, but the process was slow. By 1996 about 40 per cent of the planned social housing had been built; but large areas were still used for car parking (an unattractive but lucrative use), while the supposedly temporary collection of shops, bars and restaurants at Gabriel's Wharf was still there. CSCB have also made a number of important achievements, notably the laying out of Bernie Spain Gardens beside the OXO Tower. The gardens are named in memory of the partner of CSCB's chief executive, who died in an accident while walking in the Scottish mountains. CSCB have also converted the OXO Tower from a wharf to a mix of bijou shops, a very expensive restaurant and the most coveted low-cost rented accommodation on the south side of the Thames.

Office building has continued in the area but generally it has been on a small and medium scale. There are a variety of tenants: finance and insurance houses such Price Waterhouse Coopers on Union Street and Motability Finance on Southwark Bridge Road have spilled across the river from the City. Other banks, such as HSBC and Lloyds, have also recently opened new offices. Other important public or semi-public bodies in the area include the railway operator Connex, the Health and Safety Executive and the National Grid.

POPULATION, HOUSING AND SOCIETY

The Abercrombie Plan proposed a reduction of 50 per cent in the area's prewar population, setting a target of about 20,000. To begin with, population reduction happened naturally – if being unable to return to a bombed out home can be called natural. People moved away partly because Council policy was to re-house those on the Council waiting list outside the area, and partly because shorter working hours and greater overall prosperity gave people the freedom to live further away and travel to and from their place of work. By 1951 the population was about 22,000; in 1961, it was 17,000 and by 1991 it had fallen to about 6,500 – a density of about 54 to the acre compared to Abercrombie's aim of 136. In 1991 unemployment levels were at 12 per cent.

In the postwar period the Borough Council and the Corporation of London began a vigorous campaign of council-house building. A number of sites had been cleared by enemy action during the war, generous central government subsidies were available and the public expected the state take a lead in providing quality affordable housing for all. Many of the Southwark Borough Council flats were built on bomb sites, such as Amigo House in Morley Street and Quentin House in Gray Street. But unfortunately some of the council schemes in Bankside and St George's Fields caused the demolition of buildings of historical and architectural interest and were dismissive of their wider environment. The most notorious example was the building of the Southwark Council estate that surrounds Nelson Square. The square contained the finest group of Georgian houses in the area (excepting West Square) and these were swept aside in the early 1950s to make way for bland brick blocks. One surprising survival of postwar rebuilding is a handful of prefabs, which still stand on the north side of Borough Road.

The Corporation of London also added to its housing stock, building Bazeley House on Library Street. The Peabody Trust also made improvements to its housing, modernising the blocks on Blackfriars Road in 1956-61 and again in 1988-98 and those on Southwark Street in 1961-67. Peabody also built new accommodation in Webber Row and Keyworth Street and acquired tenement blocks built by others – for example, they bought the blocks on Marshalsea Road in 1970. Today other trusts and voluntary bodies also provide housing in the area – for example, the Salvation Army has a block called Friars Close on Bear Lane.

In the 1980s the London Borough of Southwark (successor to the Metropolitan Borough of Southwark) built Falcon Point, which stands on the riverfront between Tate Modern and Blackfriars Road, and on the site of the former Queen's Buildings (pulled down in 1978) built the Scovell Estate. The Courage site on Park Street was redeveloped in the same way. By 1991, 86 per cent of residents lived in purpose-built flats; 57 per cent rented their home from the Council, and only 4 per cent were owner-occupiers.

However, he issue of the lack of open spaces was hardly tackled. There was occasional opportunistic re-use of some sites vacated by the closure and demolition of buildings – most notably the Evelina Children's Hospital, which was converted into an adventure playground. Today many open spaces are undergoing improvement with new play areas, seats and planting. A section of Geraldine Mary Harmsworth Park has been made into a Tibetan Peace Garden and was opened by the Tibetan leader in exile, the Dalai Lama, during a visit in 1999. The opening up of the riverside has made open space available. This is attractively landscaped, and the green around Tate Modern is particularly welcome.

RELIGION, RECREATION AND EDUCATION

The fall in the local resident population has led to the closure of many churches, pubs and schools. The majority of the Anglican churches built in the later part of the 19th century closed. St Paul, Westminster Bridge Road, was badly damaged by World War II bombs and was demolished in 1957; St Peter's, Sumner Street, and All Hallows, Copperfield Street, were also the victims of wartime bombing. St Jude, Westminster Bridge Road, was converted into a community centre. St Alphege's building was demolished but its parish functions continue in what was its church hall in King's Bench Walk.

The Oxo Tower from Bernie Spain Gardens.

Two prominent churches have been rebuilt in the postwar period: St George's Cathedral and Christ Church. Work on the cathedral started in 1953 under the designs and direction of architect Romilly Craze. Given the extent of its wartime damage, there is much new work, including the day chapel, though it is all in sympathy with Pugin's Gothic style. The result is spacious and light. The major concession to economy is the incomplete west tower. The cathedral was reopened in 1958. During the rebuilding Amigo Hall – named after the much-loved Archbishop Peter Amigo, who was Bishop, later Archbishop, 1904-49 – improvised as the Cathedral Church.

Christ Church is more obviously a victim of economy. It was rebuilt in 1960 in brick to designs of R Paxton Watson & B Costin. The church has stayed active within its community and a major focus of its work has been its use as the headquarters, since 1967, of the South London Industrial Mission, established after World War II to bring the Christian faith into the workplace. Many local businesses and industries, along with the mission and other institutions, are represented in Christ Church's fine stained glass.

Webber Street and Copperfield Street schools closed. The latter became a Southwark Council training centre and is now the Jerwood Space Arts Centre. The public libraries on Borough Road and Southwark Bridge Road also closed.

Much of the 1980s were an unhappy time for the district. Unemployment was high. In addition the local Council was at times in chronic and bitter conflict with central government, which the Council saw as utterly unsympathetic to the area's needs.

One institution that did expand throughout this period was Borough Polytechnic, now South Bank University. It built a new main building on Borough Road in 1930 and developed its classes in mechanical and electrical engineering. To support the work of the local food industry, it also started a bakery school. After World War II, there was some departure from its roots, with increasingly academic courses such as physics, although the applied courses continued to dominate, with the introduction of heating engineering and the expansion of food sciences. In 1945 the poly was unkindly labelled "the university of the slums" by a national newspaper.

In 1970 the Borough Polytechnic merged with four other kindred educational establishments in south London and became the dominant partner in the newly named South Bank Polytechnic. New buildings were added in the postwar period, notably in 1953 and 1960-62, but this process accelerated. In 1983, despite opposition from Southwark Council, it opened what it called a "technopark", to train and support the work of entrepreneurs in computing, microelectronics and biotechnology. By the early 1990s the poly had expanded to its present roll of 19,000 students. Increasing numbers of these do not come from the area and so there has also been an expansion in the accommodation provided – for example, the hall of residence on the site of the Eye Hospital, which opened in 1998. In 1992, along with other polytechnics, South Bank became a University. It still holds to its original roots, with a high proportion of students living at home; contemporary but applied courses such as planning; and a wide range of teaching levels from postgraduate to diploma.

Southwark College, the local further education college, has one of its sites in The Cut. The college was formed in 1991 by the merger of Southwark College of Further Education and the Southwark Sixth Form Centre. It runs courses at Btech and NVQ level and its Waterloo site specialises in languages, management and tourism.

REGENERATION

HOUSING, TOURISM, TATE MODERN AND ATTRACTIONS

Recent developments have been in reaction to the decline in industry and the fall in population. A marked change in housing policy away from local authority provision towards private ownership has been prompted by changes in central government policy, in the ideas of the Council locally, in the views of the general public – more of whom have aspired to own their homes – and in the attitude of the private sector, which has been more prepared to invest in the area. The two most important factors have been the Council adopting a policy of stopping and substantially reversing the decline in the area's population, and private sector developers' recognition of the attractiveness to modern residents of the area's location.

Since about 1990 developers have sought to build high-quality apartments for sale or rent at prices that reflect their central location, residents' affluence and developers' substantial investment. The new developments have proved attractive to successful urban professionals enjoying the early years of a career and a single lifestyle. Some of them are purpose-built, such as the block at the corner of Union Street and Great Guildford Street, but many are conversions of previous industrial buildings, typically warehouses. The most conspicuous contribution of this sort is Bankside Lofts, a splash of bright colour developed by Manhattan Lofts to designs of CZWG, on a site near Tate Modern. The development uses part of an existing building and some new build. Benbow House, another housing development immediately to the east of the Globe Theatre, sold out as soon as it went on sale, and long before its completion. Its developer, Chelsfield, is one of the leaders in the area and anticipated investing £100 million locally.

The population has risen over the last five years and stands at about 9,100, a figure that includes about 2,000 students. It is thought that by 2010 in excess of 10,000 people will be living in the area. Commenting on the area's current population, one wry observer has noted that to live in Bankside today one needs to be very rich or very poor.

The other key factor in the change in Bankside's fortunes is tourism. In the 1980s the Council was hostile to the idea of opening up the area to visitors. Despite this, some attractions were established, notably Sam Wannamaker's Museum of the Shakespearean Stage in Bear Gardens and the Bankside Gallery, which opened in 1980; the huge King's Reach development included a hotel. This development failed and the building was converted to offices that are now occupied by Seacon. However, the increase in international travel and the tourism overload suffered by the West End and the City has seen new areas come onto the tourist map.

Landmarks in the acceptance of tourism in Bankside were the opening up of the Thames Walkway, which provided attractive open space, and the building of the Globe Theatre, which ensured that an important element of the area's history would be cherished. The Queen's Silver Jubilee Walkway – part of a walk around many districts of central London – for the first time gave continuous access to much of the Southwark riverfront. Opened in 1977, it made developers and others aware of the area's potential for visitors, culture and recreation. While Coin Street empowered local people, the rebuilding of the Globe stimulated the idea of culture- and heritage-led attractions.

Sam Wanamaker's Shakespeare's Globe Theatre.

The Globe and Rose Theatres

American actor Sam Wanamaker was fired by the desire to rebuild the Globe Theatre on Bankside almost from the first time he became acquainted with the area in the 1950s; from the early 1970s onwards, he worked towards his goal of a major centre in the area dedicated to William Shakespeare and his works. Initial progress was good – a Trust was established, property in Bankside was acquired, the Council were supportive and, by 1973, the idea had borne its first fruit in the Museum of the Shakespearean Stage in Bear Gardens. Financial problems developed, however, and there was conflict with developers, who were competing for sites in the area, and with the North Southwark Community Development Group (NSCDG), who saw the plans for a rebuilt Globe Theatre as being at variance with the needs of "the traditional working-class community of North Southwark", whose interests they represented. The NSCDG dismissed the plans as "fripperies".

In the early 1980s a site of suitable size and location on the riverfront became available and the Trust secured what it thought was the go-ahead. However, the new Council elected in 1982 was strongly supportive of the NSCDG's views and did all they could to frustrate the Globe's progress. The matter went to court in 1986 and the Globe won. Construction, working to plans drawn up by architect Theo Crosby and based on the best available evidence as to what the original theatre was like, started shortly after, but came to a halt with the discovery by archaeologists of the nearby Rose and, shortly after, the Globe itself, on Park Street. These two finds greatly influenced the final design of the modern Globe, which was completed by 1996. Sadly, Wanamaker did not live to see its official opening; he died in 1993. Although the project is the work of many hands: architects, theatre experts, archaeologists, wealthy benefactors and supporters, it was Wanamaker's relentless drive and stubbornness that saw it through.

The centre is far from complete. When finished, it will include two theatres, the Globe and another to designs of Inigo Jones; a major educational centre – educational work has always been at the heart of the project; and a large exhibition centre. Its focus, however, is the main theatre, in which plays of the Shakespearean era are performed in an environment and style that the original authors and audiences would – hopefully – recognise.

The remains of the Elizabethan Rose Theatre were discovered in 1989 during an archaeological dig during the first stages of the redevelopment of Southbridge House at Rose Alley, just west of Southwark Bridge. The find was unusual in that the theatre's "footprint" was wholly within the site, so giving unprecedented information as to its size and shape. (It was particularly important as the remains of the original Globe lie partly under Anchor Terrace, and Southwark Bridge Road and so are unlikely ever be excavated in their entirety, and the remains of the Swan were destroyed during the building of Sampson House, near Holland Street.) The Rose site became something of a shrine for the theatre world and there were calls for an extension to the dig period to allow further research and for its preservation. These were not warmly greeted by the developers, who wished to see their plans, which would have put huge foundations through the remains, built to their original timetable. The issue generated a great deal of public interest and after a campaign that involved such celebrated theatrical names as Dame Judi Dench and Sir John Gielgud, the site was made a Scheduled Ancient Monument and the new building's foundations were redesigned to avoid the remains. The remains were preserved in an inert sand cap covered with concrete, and through the efforts of the Rose Theatre Trust, the public have access to them.

Two people who have played an important role in the changes in recent times are American. They are Sam Wanamaker, the driving force behind the rebuilding of Shakespeare's Globe Theatre on Bankside, and Southwark Council's director of Development, Fred Manson. It is reasonable to speculate that fresh eyes and no respect for established and inertia-filled ways of working brought results.

It is particularly exciting that the Bankside area is developing without reference to a rigid master-plan. The changes are among the most dynamic in London and will continue for many years to come. The process is led by the private sector and encouraged by the London Borough of Southwark, until 1999 the Government Office for London and thereafter the Greater London Authority and the Cross River Partnership. Effecting change is a delicate balancing act, reconciling the needs of employers, residents current and future, and visitors. Local residents' views are represented through the active Bankside Residents' Forum. Other bodies involved in the area are the Bankside Business Partnership, which represents the large employers, the Bankside Traders' Association, which represents smaller traders and shops and the Bankside Marketing Group, which represents the visitor attractions.

TATE MODERN AND OTHER ATTRACTIONS

The crowning achievement has been Tate Modern. The conversion of Bankside power station into a new home for the Tate Gallery's modern collection was particularly appropriate because of the area's existing artistic community; it also put a former industrial building to imaginative use and throughout the process involved local residents in planning the changes. The conversion was a happy solution to a two-headed problem: the Tate Gallery's main site on Millbank needed a new home for its modern collection; the

*The turbine hall of Bankside Power Station during conversion
into Tate Modern.*

authorities had encountered great difficulties in re-developing the
power station site because although power generation had ceased
in 1981 the site was – and still is – used as a switching station,
making demolition difficult and dangerous. The Tate was
encouraged by a positive and Council-funded feasibility study and
a sale price for the site of just £12 million. Work on converting
the building started in 1995 and was complete in May 2000. The
conversion was to designs of Swiss architects Herzog + de Meuron
and their project architect Harry Gugger.

Building was more difficult and involved than originally envisaged,
notably in the roof, most of which had to be replaced; there were
also problems with the delivery and fitting of major elements of the
building. Herzon + de Meuron's plans were in sympathy with the

building's previous use but the final designs were made in conjunction with Tate staff and trustees, who were involved in the smallest details, and the engineers and project managers, who had to ensure it would work and be in budget. This group was led and held together by Sir Nicholas Serota, director of the Tate Gallery. The conversion cost a mere £134 million – much less than the cost of a new building of a comparable size, and one-fifth of the cost of the Millennium Dome. The Tate Gallery was at pains to work with the local community during the building work and thereafter, and have set up the Bankside Artists Training Trust to support young artists working locally.

The development is very impressive: its cavernous turbine hall overwhelms visitors by its vast space – it is 500 feet long, 100 feet high and 80 feet wide (150 by 30 by 25 metres); giant oriel light boxes high on the turbine hall walls are both witty and provide visitors on the balconies behind with spectacular views. There have also been criticisms: the grand staircase is too hard to find and too enclosed to be genuinely "grand" and the decision to display the collection thematically rather than by style or period disappointed some. The permanent collection is displayed over two floors, with another floor and the turbine hall used for temporary displays. One of the building's great strengths is that almost as much space is given over to space for people to circulate, relaxation, refreshment and commerce as to exhibition.

The Tate knew that the public were traditionally hesitant about modern art, and has been surprised by the success of the new gallery. Estimates of 2 million visitors in the first year were far surpassed – the figure was closer to 5 million. It has been estimated it will generate 2,400 jobs locally. In terms of modern art galleries across the world, London can now compare with those in New York, the Getty in Los Angeles and the Guggenheim in Bilbao.

Tate Modern has many parallels with Southwark Cathedral: its proportions, the use of vertical decoration, a central tower and west door are all superficial physical similarities; both are public places for introspection and contemplation and both are products of their day, the Cathedral a place dedicated to piety and intercession and the gallery a place of industry and now recreation.

Tate Modern does not have a monopoly of the cultural sector in the area. One of the factors that attracted the Tate to Bankside was the thriving community of artists working locally. This community supported smaller scale galleries in the area such as the Royal Watercolour Society and the Royal Society of Painter-Printmakers at Bankside Gallery under Falcon Point from 1980 onwards. A more recent addition, and one more in keeping with the avantgarde work of local artists, was the Jerwood Foundation on Union Street. This has its home in a converted London School Board School and opened in 1998. The complex has gallery and rehearsal space. The commercial "SE1 Gallery" on Southwark Street and "Purdy Hicks Gallery" in Hopton Street are other new additions.

Other cultural attractions in the area include a replica of the *Golden Hinde* ship, which is moored in St Mary Overie dock; the long-established Clink Prison Museum, which is in the basement of a Victorian warehouse and tells the story of the medieval Clink prison, which was nearby; and the sleek and commercial Vinopolis, an ambitious display, housed in the railway arches of the line to Cannon Street, of the history and culture of wine. Away from Bankside proper, the Fire Brigade has a display on its history at its old headquarters on Southwark Bridge Road, and the Imperial War Museum continues to expand its displays, most recently with the Holocaust Museum.

Evidence of the area's history can be found in many places. Southwark Cathedral is the most distinguished, recently enhanced by a new visitor centre. At the Rose Theatre the shape of the remains of the theatre are skilfully projected onto their concrete case. Nearby are the excavated foundations and 14th-century rose window of the Great Hall of the Bishop of Winchester's palace. There are a good number of 18th-century houses away from the river on Union Street, and two very old domestic houses, which vie for the title of the oldest in the area. One is 61 Hopton Street of c.1702 and the other is 49 Bankside, which probably dates from the late 17th century. At 49 Bankside the apparently ancient plaque that bears extravagant claims for the residence there of Sir Christopher Wren in fact dates from after World War II; there is no evidence, nor any realistic likelihood, that Wren really lived there. The pair of brick terraced houses next door, now the lodging of the Dean of Southwark Cathedral, dates from 1712. Even Southwark's industrial history is not forgotten as the Kirkaldy testing works at 99 Southwark Street has a museum that includes the testing equipment.

The theatres in the area add another cultural dimension. The Globe concentrates on the performance of Elizabethan and Jacobean plays in their original context: daylight open-air performances, few props and a standing audience who are encouraged to interact with the performance. The Southwark Playhouse on Southwark Bridge Road is more rooted in the community, involving local schools and the wider history of the area in many of its productions. The Union Theatre in Union Street is smaller and more experimental.

Visitor numbers have expanded significantly, from 2 million in 1998 to 5.5 million in 2000. Hotels and restaurants have opened to serve them. There are more than 500 beds in the area's three hotels and this number is set to rise in the future. There are also many new restaurants. The first high-quality arrival was "Livebait" on The Cut, and it set the standard for others. Not all new eating places are expensive – it is possible to spend one-tenth of the amount one would in an upmarket eatery and still dine well. With the closure of many traditional pubs a drinking environment of dark wood and hand pumps has been largely replaced by the chrome, bleached wood, bottles and neon blue of new bars.

Public architecture is also part of the process of regeneration in both buildings and – less obviously – streetscaping. The practice Muf laid a pavement surface of Thames shingle and built a black concrete bench on part of Southwark Street, creating a so-called "urban beach"; the word Bankside appears as a slogan in huge lettering at various locations, at once branding the district and redefining its historic boundaries – to the disadvantage of the equally distinguished area of The Borough. The river walk has been extended and remodelled with underpasses beneath all the bridges, a carved mural on green slate depicting the history of the area under Southwark Bridge and refashioning of the section near the Globe. St George's Circus has been remodelled and the obelisk, first erected there in 1770 and removed in 1905, was put back in place in 1996. Sadly, however, away from the riverfront the quality of the pedestrian environment is poor.

THE JUBILEE LINE AND THE MILLENNIUM BRIDGE

The most striking new building is also a public one: Southwark Station. The line it serves, the Jubilee Line of the London Underground, connects north Southwark with the West End and east London, a corridor of commercial activity including Canary Wharf and developments to the east of London Bridge. The Jubilee Line is unusual in that it is a major part of the regeneration of the inner-city rather than, as with many lines, the catalyst for the development of a suburb. The idea for a new underground line to the east of London had been circulating since the late 1970s, but the scheme did not get the go-ahead until 1993. Its construction took much longer and was much more expensive than originally planned. Even the supposedly immovable opening date of 31 December 1999, when the line was to carry the "great and the good" to the New Year's Eve celebrations at the Millennium Dome, was seriously in doubt.

In the stations and other buildings that serve the line, London Underground, to its credit, has recognised the need for buildings of quality that will endure and provide travellers with an aesthetically pleasing environment. The senior Jubilee Line architect Roland Paoletti appointed a different architectural practice for each station. Southwark was designed by MacCormac Jamieson Prichard. It uses an iconic tube design for its circular station building and then breaks from tradition with an underground concourse lit by natural light let in by a huge skylight. On one side of the concourse are escalators to the platforms and on the other, confronting travellers as they ascend the escalators, is a 130-foot (40-metre) long curved wall of triangular panels of blue glass.

Competing with Southwark Station as the finest visual addition to the area is the Millennium Bridge. This is the first new bridge over the Thames in London since Tower Bridge of 1894. It is a footbridge that runs from Tate Modern to St Paul's Cathedral and symbolically places Bankside at the very centre of London once again. The bridge is a sleek, low, steel structure designed by Sir Norman Foster, Anthony Caro and the engineers Ove Arup; Foster said it was inspired by a blade of light from a children's cartoon of his youth. As well as being visually stunning, particularly when lit at night, its design is technically adventurous – a suspension bridge whose suspending cables barely rise above the walkway. Sadly, it suffered the fate of many millennium projects as it was not complete at the time of its official opening in May 2000 and was closed very shortly afterwards because it was found to oscillate in step with crossing pedestrians. Once this is resolved and the bridge reopened, it will be a landmark and link of the first order, binding Bankside to central London.

THE FUTURE

Bankside still faces many challenges. A massive increase in visitor numbers has to be reconciled with the needs of local residents. New residents must not cause the sharp polarisation between "haves" and "have nots" that was the case with many of the redevelopments in Docklands. The redevelopment of large sites needs to be handled sensitively. St Christopher House on Southwark Street, Orbit House on Blackfriars Road and the site above the Southwark underground station are all to be developed. Not all employment can be taken for granted; J.Sainsbury recently announced they are leaving the area for Holborn, removing 4,000 jobs and releasing £100 million of assets. There are major proposals to widen the railway viaduct carrying trains from London Bridge to Blackfriars, which would destroy many of the older buildings near the Cathedral.

For all of these uncertainties Bankside's future – because of Tate Modern and the Jubilee Line – is secure. The area presents an exciting mix of buildings of all types and dates; there are surprising survivals from many periods. There is also an exciting mix of people: university students, office workers, barristers and solicitors, firemen, journalists, printers, scrap-metal dealers, chefs, and long-established and recently arrived residents. What is most satisfying from a historian's point of view is that Bankside's history is playing a real role in the area's regeneration. It may be that for the last 1,000 years the area has been important for things most people did not want to associate themselves with, but this is not the case now. Bankside is forging its own sense of identity, one that places it confidently where is deserves to be, at the heart of London.

BOOKLIST

Boast, Mary *The story of Bankside*. L.B. Southwark, 1985.

Survey of London Vol. XXV *St George's Fields*. LCC, 1955.

Survey of London Vol. XXII *Bankside*. LCC, 1950.

London Encyclopaedia. Ed Ben Weinreb and Christopher Hibbert Macmillan, 1987.

Pevsner, Nikolaus & Cherry, Bridget *London South*. Buildings of England, Penguin 1983.

Reilly, Leonard *Southwark an Illustrated History*. London Borough of Southwark 1998.

Carlin, Martha *Medieval Southwark*. Hambledon Press, 1996.

Golden, Grace *Old Bankside*. Williams & Northgate, 1950.

Carrington R C *Two schools. A history of St Olave's and St Saviour's School*. The school governors, 1971.

Evans F G V *Borough Polytechnic* 1892-1969. Borough Polytechnic, 1969.

Humphrey Stephen *A guide to the archives in Southwark Local Studies Library*. London Borough of Southwark, 1992

LCC *The housing Question in London* four volumes, 1900, 1928, 1931, 1937.

Johnson, David *Southwark and the City*. Oxford Univeristy Press 1969.

Time Out *Guide to Bankside & Tate Modern,* 2000.

More, Rowan and Ryan Raymund, *Buildng Tate Modern*. Tate Gallery 2000.

Sabbagh, *Karl Power into Art*. Penguin 2000.

Williams, Bridget *The best butter in the world. A history of Sainsbury's*. Ebury Press, 1994.

Inwood Stephen, *A History of London*. Macmillan, 1998.

Southwark Cathedral [Guide to the Cathedral] Southwark Cathedral and Jarrold, 1990.

Annual reports and Medical Officer of Health Reports of the vestries of Christ Church and St George the Martyr and the St Saviour Board of Works.

Harris, Harry, *Under Oars*. Centerprise, 1978.

Cole, Harry, *Policemans Prelude*. Fontana, 1987.

Mackinder, Anthony and Blatherwick, Simon, *Bankside: excavations at Benbow House, Southwark*. Museum of London Archaeology Service 1999.

Day, Barry, *This Wooden'O' Shakespeare's Globe reborn*. Oberon 1996.

INDEX

Abercrombie Plan   118, 119

Adams, James, engineer   59

administration   13-14, 18-19,
63-5, 78, 83

agriculture   15, 36, 55

air raids   104, 113, 114,
116-7, 128

Albion Mills   57

All Hallows Church,
Copperfield Street   94, 128

almshouses   32, 70

Alleyn, Edward   21, 24, 26

Anchor Brewery   48-51, 109
see also Barclay Perkins

Andrews, Launcelot   9

artists and art galleries 125, 130,
132, 135-8

Ashby, James,
tea packers   57, 123

Association of
Waterloo Groups   125-6
see also Coin Street Community
Builders

Astley's circus and theatre   101

Austral Street   87

Bakerloo Railway line   109

Bankside   10, 138, 139

Bankside Gallery   132, 138

Bankside Gas Works   53

Bankside Lofts   132

Bankside Marketing Group   135

Bankside Power Station   53-4,
112-3, 118-120, 135-6

Bankside Residents' Forum   135

Bankside Traders' Association 135

Barclay and Fry, printers   61

Barclay Perkins & Co   49-51,
103, 109-110, 123

bear baiting   24-6

Bear Gardens   26, 29, 132-3

Bear Lane   42, 74

Benbow House   132

Bermondsey Abbey   14

Bernie Spain Gardens   126

Bethlem Hospital   66-7, 107-8
see also Imperial War Museum

Bishop of Winchester   8, 9, 15,
19, 27, 96

Bishop of Winchester's
Manor see Clink

Bishop of Winchester's Palace
see Winchester Palace

Blackfriars Bridge   38-9, 41

Blackfriars Crown Court   125

Blackfriars Road   39, 42, 80

Blackfriars Settlement   85-6

Blackfriars Type Foundry   125

Blomfield, Sir Arthur   9

Boards of Guardians 63, 83, 105,
106-7, 115

Booth, Charles   78

Borough Polytechnic 55, 92-3, 130
see also South Bank Polytechnic
and South Bank University

Borough Road   38, 75, 78, 97-8

boundary marks   65

Bowers, Robert, printer
and writer   61

Bowler, Thomas, hat maker   60-1

boxing   26, 108

Boyfield Street   45, 81

brewing   11, 26, 48-53, 109-110

Bridewell Palace   89

Bridge House Estate
and Committee   18, 36, 37, 43,
44-5, 106
see also City of London

bridges
        Blackfriars Bridge   38, 41
        London Bridge   6, 57
        Millennium Bridge   109, 140

St Paul's Bridge 109

Southwark Bridge 40, 57, 109, 139

Waterloo Bridge 39, 57

Westminster Bridge 37

Bridge Ward Without 18

British and Foreign School Society 89, 90

Broadwall 10, 35

brothels 19-21
see also stews

bull baiting 24-6

Burbage, Cuthbert and Richard 21

Burghal hideage 6

burial grounds 76, 82, 85

Burrups, printers 62, 114-5

Calvert's Buildings 52

Cathedral School 89

charities 32, 34, 66-71, 85-7
see also almshouses

Charlotte Sharman's Children's Home 86-7

Charlotte Sharman School 87, 91

children's homes 83, 86-7

cholera 75-6, 84

Christ Church 34, 94, 129-30

Christ Church Parochial School 33

Church Commissioners 81, 106

churches and chapels
All Hallows, Copperfield Street 94, 128
Christ Church, 34, 94, 129-30
Priory of St Mary Overie 7-8
see also St Saviour;'s Church and Southwark Cathedral
St Alphege 62, 94-6, 128
St George's Cathedral 98, 99, 129
St George the Martyr 94

St Jude, St George's Road 94, 128

St Margaret 9

St Mary Magdalen 9

St Michael and All Angels, Lant Street 94

St Paul, Westminster Bridge Road 94

St Peter's Sumner Street 94, 128

St Saviour 8-9, 24
see also Priory of St Mary Overie and Southwark Cathedral

St Thomas

Southwark Cathedral 9, 53, 97, 137, 138
see also Priory of St Mary Overie and Southwark Cathedral

Stamford Street Unitarian Chapel 97

Surrey Chapel 97, 108

Union Street Independent Chapel 97

Welsh Congregational Chapel 97-8

circuses 101

City of London 13, 17, 18-19, 20, 21, 36, 37, 63, 64, 67, 76, 105-6, 119, 127

Civil war 32

clinics 107

Clink, manor of 10, 14, 15-16, 18, 19-21

Clink Prison 15, 36, 138

Clink Street 6

Cole, Harry 106, 107

Coin Street 125-6

Coin Street Community Builders 125-6

Copt Hall 34

Copperfield Street 75

Copperfield Street School *see* Orange Street School

Corporation of Wardens of St Saviour   64, 71

Costermongers   62

Craze, Romilly   129

crime   15, 17, 20, 99

Crosby, Theo   134

Cross Bones Burial Ground   82

crown glass   29-30

Cure's College   32

Cut, The   40, 62

CZWG, architects   132

Deadman's Place   16, 29

Davenport, J T   56

death rates   75, 106-7

Dickens, Charles   78

disease   75-6

Dog and Duck, spa and tavern   32, 36, 37, 42, 67, 70, 100-1

Dogget's Coat and Badge race   11

Doyle, Fr Thomas

drainage   10, 39, 45, 46, 76, 85 *see also* sewers

Drapers' Company almshouses 70

Dulwich College   24

Easton and Amos, engineers   58

electricity generation 53-4, 112-3

embankments   10

engineering   57-60, 113-4

Epps Cocoa   57

Express Newspapers   125

Evelina Children's Hospital   83

Eye Hospital *see* Royal Eye Hospital

Falcon Glassworks   31

Falcon Inn   27

Fegan's Homes   87

Financial Times   125

Finch's Grotto   100-1

fires   8, 10, 27

Fire Brigade   93-4, 138

Fishmongers' Company almshouses   70

fishponds   11

Flora Gardens   101

food industry   11, 47, 48, 55-7, 109-112, 123

Foster, Sir Norman, architect 140

Freemasons' School   70

Frost Fairs   27

gas works   53

Geraldine Mary Harmsworth Park   108, 128

glassmaking   28-31

Globe Theatre   21, 23, 132-5, 139

Golden, Grace   121

Gordon riots   37, 49-50

Goulden, Rev Alfred   95-6

Gower, John   9

Grand Vitesse railway depot   42

Gravel Lane   35

Great Suffolk Street   15, 35

Great Surrey Street   39

Greater London Council

Green Walk   35, 42

Grey and Martin, lead works,   113-4

Grottos, the and Grotto Place, 75, 81, 85

Gugger, Harry, architect   135-7

Guildable Manor

Gun Street   45, 81

Gwilt, George   8-9

Halsey, Edmund   48-9

Harris, Harry   114

Harvard, John 9
hat making 60-1
Haynau, General 51
Hayward Brothers, engineers 59
Hedger family 37, 42-5, 100
Henslowe, Philip 21, 23, 26
Herzog + de Meuron,
architects 135-7
Hill, Octavia 81
Hill, Rowland 97
Hollands Leaguer 20
Hope Theatre 21, 26
Hopton's Almshouses 70
Hopton Street 5, 35, 138
Hop and Malt Exchange 52,123
hop trade 51-2, 110, 121-3
hospitals 7, 83
Horseshoe Alley Stairs 40
horsepower 51
hotels 61, 139
housing 42, 46, 73-5, 78, 79-81,
105-6, 127-8, 131-2

immigration 13, 72
Imperial War Museum 104, 138
industries 13, 27-32, 47-62,
109-115, 118-124
IPC Magazines 125

Jerwood Foundation
and Space 130, 138
Johnson, Ben 23
Johnson, Dr Samuel 49, 50
Jubilee Line 140, 141

Keyworth, Leonard 104
King Edward's School 88-9
King's Bench Prison 36
King's Bench Street 81
King's Manor 14

Kirkaldy, David 58, 139
Lancaster, Joseph 90
leather trade 11
libraries 93
lighters and
lightermen 11-12, 47, 114
London Bridge 6, 57
London Borough
of Southwark 130, 135
London, Chatham
and Dover Railway 41, 72
London County Council 63, 81,
91, 92-3, 105, 115, 119
London Cycling Campaign 124
London Hydraulic
Power Company 47-8, 54
London School Board 63, 91
London, City of see City of London

MacCormac Jamieson
Prichard, architects 140
Maid or Maiden Lane 11, 19, 35
Magdalen Hospital
for Penitent Prostitutes 68, 80
manors 10,14, 64
    Clink 10,14, 15-16, 18
    Guildable 14
    King's 14
    Paris Garden 10, 14, 17, 20
market gardening 55
markets 44, 62
Marlowe, Christopher 23, 24
Marshall, John 34
Marshalsea Road 41
Marygold Stairs 38
Massey Shaw, Capt 94
Max & Co., printers 61
Medical Officers
of Health 77, 78-9, 99
Metropolitan Board
of Works 40, 63, 85, 93-4

Metropolitan Borough
of Southwark   65, 104, 105,
                      106-7, 119
Millennium Bridge   109, 140
model dwelling companies 79-81
monotorial system   90
Morley College   93
Moulstrand Dock   11
Muf, architects   139
music halls   101-2
Mylne, Robert   38

National Society   89
Nelson Square   42, 55, 73,
                      85, 86, 127
Newcomen Schools   33,89
Nonconformist churches
and chapels   16, 97
North Southwark Community
Development Group   133-4
Notre Dame Girls' School 90-1

Obelisk   39, 140
offices   124, 126
Old Barge House Brewery   51
Orbit House   124, 141
Orange Street School 91, 130
Oxo Company
and tower   103, 111-2, 126

Pakeman House   106
Paris Garden, manor of 10, 17, 20
Park Street   6, 35
parks and open spaces 85, 108,
                      119, 128
parochial schools   33, 89
Pascalls, confectioners   55
paving commissioners 64
Peabody Buildings
and Trust   80, 127
Peacock Brewery   51

Pellatt, Apsley   31
Perkins, Henry and John   44, 49
Philanthropic Society 68-70
Phoenix Gas Works
poor law and relief 63, 79, 82, 83
see also Boards of Guardians
population   12-13, 71-2, 105, 132
poverty   77-8
printing   61-2, 114-5, 118, 123-5
Priory of St Mary Overie   7-8
see also St Saviour's Church
and Southwark Cathedral
prostitution   19-21, 100, 101
public baths   85
public health   75-6, 78, 82-5, 107
pubs   26-7, 45, 101-2
Pugin, A W   98

Queen's Buildings   80, 106, 128

railways   41-2, 70, 72-3, 109, 140
recreation 19-27, 36, 100-2, 107-8
Red Cross Cottages   81
Reformation   16
Rendle, William   77, 100
Rennie, John and Sir John 57
restaurants   139
Ring, The   108
river stairs   12, 39, 40
Roman Catholicism   16, 37, 98
Romans   5-6
Rose Theatre   21, 23, 134-5, 138
Rotunda, the   91-2
Royal Barge House   12
Royal Eye Hospital   83, 101

Sainsbury, J, food
merchants   55, 110-1, 123, 141
St Alphege's Church 62, 94-6, 128
St Christopher House 124, 141

St George's Cathedral 98, 99, 129

St George's Circus   38-9, 45, 139

St George's Fields   14, 32, 35-9,
                      42-6, 66, 76

St Jude's Church,
St George's Road   94, 128

St Margaret's Church   9

St Mary Magdalen's Church   9

St Mary Overie Dock   11, 138

St Mary Overy's Wharf   47

St Michaels and All Angel's
Church, Lant Street   94

St Olave's Grammar School   10

St Paul's Bridge   109

St Paul's Church,
Westminster Bridge Road 94, 128

St Peter's Church,
Sumner Street   94, 128

St Saviour's Board of Works   63

St Saviour's Church   8-9, 24

see also Priory of St Mary Overie
and Southwark Cathedral

St Saviour's
Grammar School   10, 33, 88-9

St Stephen's
Parliamentary Press   123-4

St Thomas' Hospital   7

Sanctuaries   17

School for the
Indigent Blind   70

schools

    Cathedral School   89

    Charlotte Sharman
    School   87, 91

    Christ Church
    arochial School   33

    Freemasons' School   70

    King Edward's School   88-9

    Newcomen Schools   33, 89

    Notre Dame,
    girls' school   90-1

    Orange Street School 91, 130

St Olave's
Grammar School   10, 88

St Saviour's
Grammar School   10, 33, 88

St Saviour's parochial
School   33

Webber Row School   91, 130

West Square School   91

see also National Society,
British and Foreign School
Society, Lancaster, Joseph,
London School Board

Scott, Sir Giles Gilbert   119

Sennett Brothers, fur cutters   60

sewers   76, 84

Shakespeare, Edmund   9

Shakespeare, William   23-4

Sharman's homes   86-7

Sisters of the Reparation,
Convent of   96

South Bank   118

South Bank Polytechnic   130-1

South Bank
University   92-3, 130-1

South Eastern Railway   41-2

South London
Industrial Mission   130

South London Palace   101-2

Southwark Bacon
Drying Company   112, 123

Southwark Borough Council
see either Metropolitan Borough
of Southwark or London
Borough of Southwark

Southwark Bridge   40, 57,
                    109, 139

Southwark Bridge Road   40

Southwark Cathedral   6, 9, 53,
                      97, 137, 138

see also Priory of St Mary Overie
and St Saviour's Church

Southwark College   131

Southwark Playhouse   121, 139
Southwark Station   140
Southwark Street   40-1, 52,
                        73, 80, 87, 139
Southwark, Diocese of   96-7
Spas   100-1
Stamford Street   42, 55, 73
Stamford Street
Unitarian Chapel   97
Stevenson and Howell,
food essence makers   123
stews   19-21
Stopher House   106
Sumner Buildings   106
Sumner Street   10, 106
Surrey Chapel   97, 108
Surrey Institution   91-2
Surrey Theatre   101
Surrey, county of   63
Swan Thetare   21, 23

Tate Modern   118, 128
                         135-137, 141
Temple-West family   44-5
theatres   19, 21-6, 133-5, 139
Thames, River   6, 11-12, 47,
                        107, 121, 132
Thrale, Ralph and Henry   49
Tourism   132-42
Tress & Co., hat makers   61
typhus   76

Union Street   40, 74-5, 82
Union Street
Independent Chapel   97
Union Theatre   139
Unilever   124
Upper Ground   10, 27
Upton Frederick, hat maker   60

Valentine Place   55, 56, 65
vinegar brewing   52

Wanamaker, Sam   133-5
warehouses   27-8, 47-8,
                   111, 114, 118, 120-1
war memorials   53
Waterloo Bridge   39, 57
Waterloo Road   39, 81
Watermen   19
water mills   11
water supply   75-6, 78, 84
waterworks   75-6
Webber Street   56, 75, 81
Webber Street School   91, 130
Welsh Congregational
Chapel   97-8
West Square   44, 85, 87
West Square School   91
Westminster Bridge   37-8
wharves   6, 11, 27-8, 47-8,
        111, 112, 113, 114, 120-1, 123
White Cross Cottages   81
Whitehill Houses   81
Wicks Rotary Type Casting   125
Willcox, engineers   60
Williams, Sir Owen   111
Winchester Cottages   81
Winchester House,
Southwark Bridge Road   82
see also Fire Brigade
Winchester Palace   6,15-16,
                         29, 47, 138
Winchester, Bishop of
see Bishop of Winchester
World War I   53, 103-5
World War II   113, 114,
                         116-7, 128
Workhouses   82

Zoar Street   16